WHY *Believe* THE BIBLE?

JOHN F. MACARTHUR

WHY *Believe* THE BIBLE?

BakerBooks
a division of Baker Publishing Group
Grand Rapids, Michigan

© 1980 by G/L Publications

Published by Baker Books
a division of Baker Publishing Group
P.O. Box 6287, Grand Rapids, MI 49516-6287
www.bakerbooks.com

Baker Books edition published 2015
ISBN 978-0-8010-1794-0

Previouly published in 1980 and 2007 by Regal Books

Printed in the United States of America

The Library of Congress has catalogued the first edition as follows:
MacArthur, John, 1939–
    Why believe the Bible / John F. MacArthur
        p. cm.
    ISBN 978-0-8307-4564-7 (hard cover)
    1. Bible—Evidences, authority, etc.
BS 480.M22
220.1'3—dc19   79091704

15   16   17   18   19   20   21   7   6   5   4   3   2   1

Dedicated to Bob Vernon
in gratitude for his faithful prayers
and generous friendship.

CONTENTS

PART III

HOW TO GET THE MOST FROM GOD'S WORD

PREFACE
TO THE 2015 EDITION

This book, originally published in 1980, was one of my earliest written works. At the time, I was already a full decade into my ministry at Grace Community Church. I could not have envisioned the extraordinary longevity the Lord would graciously grant me as pastor and teacher here, and I am profoundly grateful to be still serving the same congregation four and a half decades after being called here. My driving passions then, as now, were to make the Word of God known and understood to my congregation, and (even beyond the circle of our fellowship) to persuade as many people as possible that the Bible is true and trustworthy.

This book had its genesis about the same time as *Grace to You* began broadcasting Bible teaching daily on the radio across North America. My goal was to declare the authority and inerrancy of God's Word to as many ears as my voice could reach, and I therefore purposely wrote this book to be as basic and accessible as human language would permit.

In those days, the evangelical community was embroiled in a significant controversy about the authority, sufficiency, and inerrancy of the Bible. Biblical conviction was under heavy assault from liberalism and neo-orthodoxy, especially in academic circles. Some of the most prestigious evangelical seminaries had become hotbeds of compromise and even skepticism. Telltale signs in several once-sound churches and denominations revealed that even where God's Word had once been proclaimed with power and clarity, confidence in the authority and reliability of Scripture was getting wobbly. Harold Lindsell's explosive 1976 book, *The Battle for the Bible*, exposed and documented the trends.

In October 1978, a group of concerned churchmen and scholars led by James Montgomery Boice and Jay Grimstead founded the International Council on Biblical Inerrancy (ICBI). The organization drew together a hundred faithful leaders and biblical scholars who for the next decade wrote books, published papers, and united their efforts in an unprecedented way to reaffirm and defend the historic evangelical commitment to the absolute authority of Scripture.

In their early meetings together, ICBI's leadership made a list of 14 areas of debate, and they commissioned a series of white papers to answer every challenge that was being made against the truthfulness or accuracy of Scripture. Within its first decade, ICBI sponsored three summit meetings that brought together some 300 evangelical scholars to discuss and defend the principle of biblical inerrancy. The organization hosted two major national gatherings that were open to the public. And they coordinated the publication of dozens of books with numerous evangelical publishers, all in defense of the accuracy, authority, and sufficiency of the Bible.

But ICBI's most enduring contribution was the historic document reproduced here as an appendix: *The Chicago Statement on Biblical Inerrancy*. It is without rival as the most important and influential theological document of the 20th century. ICBI co-founder Jay Grimstead called it "the first systematically comprehensive, broadly based, scholarly, creed-like statement on the inspiration and authority of Scripture in the history of the church."

The work accomplished by ICBI was monumental, but the organization was founded to perform a highly focused and well-defined job, not to become an institution. So, in September 1987, when the work that was laid out at the start had been accomplished, the organization was formally disbanded.

For the next decade and a half, inerrancy was hardly a controversial issue. Relatively few overt or large-scale challenges to biblical inerrancy arose within evangelical denominations and seminaries, and those that tried received scant publicity and seemed to have little influence. But other, more subtle, threats to biblical authority *did* manage to gain footholds among evangelicals. These included overtly pragmatic methods of evangelism and church growth; a move away from biblical preaching in favor of psychology and various kinds of entertainment; and the deliberate dumbing down of content in most forms of evangelical media (radio, television, books, and magazines). Having won the hard-fought inerrancy debate, the evangelical community seemed to lose interest in the victory, choosing instead to focus attention on things other than Scripture.

Most of those in church leadership today have no memory of ICBI and the inerrancy debate. As a result, many of the old, already-answered arguments against the reliability of Scripture are resurfacing in nuanced fashion as if they constituted new and revolutionary ideas. Suddenly the inerrancy of Scripture is back on the table for debate.

It is an opportune time to bring this book back into print.

I have never aspired to be known as a theologian, a polemicist, or an academician. My main passion is teaching and preaching the Word of God. That is why I wrote this book with lay readers in mind. It is not meant to be a textbook or an academic treatise; it is just a simple, basic introduction to the Word of God, highlighting the Bible's proper role as the Christian's sole, sufficient, and final authority in all matters of faith and practice.

It is also a plea to Christians to keep a proper focus on Scripture as they try to navigate this pathologically shallow, media-hungry, entertainment-oriented, pleasure-mad, distraction-filled culture.

The attack on inerrancy today may pose a greater threat than it did 35 years ago, because Christians are now preoccupied with everything *but* the authority and truthfulness of the Word of God—and that is a profound tragedy. Even worse, many churches seem to encourage their people to be more concerned with things like stylishness, relationships, prosperity, temporal wellbeing, and other worldly cares than with the truth of Scripture. The church becomes weak and ineffectual wherever the Word of God is not proclaimed with boldness and conviction.

Here, in fact, is the primary duty of every faithful pastor: "Preach the word; be ready in season and out of season; reprove, rebuke, and exhort, with complete patience and teaching" (2 Timothy 4:2, ESV). When Paul wrote those words to Timothy, he added this prophetic warning: "The time is coming when people will not endure sound teaching, but having itching ears they will accumulate for themselves teachers to suit their own passions, and will turn away from listening to the truth and wander off into myths" (vv. 3–4).

We are living in such a time, and the only way to resist the downward pull of a declining society is by anchoring our lives in the Word of God. That means our minds must be renewed by God's truth as revealed in the Bible (Romans 12:1–2). Our thoughts, our affections, and our actions must be brought into conformity with the Word of God. That's hardly possible for those who do not know God's Word, because Scripture stands in opposition to human instinct, earthly wisdom, and worldly philosophy. "The natural person does not accept the things of the Spirit of God, for they are folly to him, and he is not able to understand them because they are spiritually discerned" (1 Corinthians 2:14, ESV).

My hope is that if you are a believer, this book will not only bolster your confidence in the authority and reliability of God's Word but also motivate you to become a student and a lover of the Bible. And if you are not yet a believer, I trust you will consider the claims of Scripture seriously, with an open heart. May the Spirit of God grant you an understanding of the things freely given to us by God.

John F. MacArthur

PART I

****

CAN WE REALLY BELIEVE THE BIBLE?

As Christians, most of us would like to say that we of course believe the Bible. But we are surrounded by a worldly secular system in which all truth is relative and in which there are no absolutes. The Bible is not openly attacked as much as it is subtly undermined. It is accepted as one more way to look at the world, but its divine authority is simply passed over, ignored, flippantly popularized or dismissed with a tolerant smile. Today more than ever, people are asking the following questions:

- *What Does God's Word Mean to Us?* Is it authoritative, infallible, inerrant and effective in our life? How can we tell?

- *Who Can Prove God's Word Is True?* What about the evidence in changed lives, the Bible's uncanny ability to keep matching up with scientific discovery, archaeological finds, fulfilled prophecy? What is the only "final proof" of the truth of Scripture?

- *How Did God Inspire His Word?* Did God use biblical writers like robots and dictate the 66 books to them? Are the writers inspired, or the writings? Or both? What does Scripture mean by "inspired"?

- *What Did Jesus Think of God's Word?* Can we believe in Christ's authority but not the authority and truthfulness of Scripture? Did Jesus support the Scripture of His day as truthful history?

- *Can You Add to God's Word?* Who decided which books would go in the Bible and which ones would not? What happens when individuals or groups try to add to the Scriptures?

In these first five chapters, we will grapple with these very old questions that are still extremely relevant today.

CHAPTER 1

WHAT DOES GOD'S WORD MEAN TO US?

How important is the Bible to people's lives?

There are several ways to answer that question. Some say, "The Bible? It's just another book. Some wise sayings here and there, mixed with a lot of genealogies, myths and crazy visions."

A second group says something like this: "Of course I know the Bible is important—at least my pastor thinks so. He's always quoting it and waving it in the air. But I don't read it too much—can't really understand it too well."

There is still a third group, however, who would align themselves with Sir Walter Scott, a famed British novelist and poet, who was also a committed Christian. On his deathbed, Scott is reported to have said to his secretary, "Bring me the Book." His secretary thought of the thousands of books in Scott's library and inquired, "Dr. Scott, which book?"

"The Book," replied Scott. "The Bible—the only book for a dying man!"

The committed Christian would have to add that the Bible is not just the only book for a dying man, but it's the only book for a living man, because it is the Word of God.

In which of the three categories do you fall? Obviously, Group 1 represents the typical response from the secular world. It doesn't know Christ, and it accepts only what seems to fit in with worldly wisdom. For them the Bible has little importance and less authority.

Group 2 includes a lot of church members, and even some Christians. They know the Bible is important and that it should have priority and authority in their lives, but they don't make much personal use of it. They neglect its teachings altogether, or they slip by, seldom opening the Bible for themselves and depend on pastors, teachers or speakers to "explain it to them." They make little application of what the Scriptures teach. The Bible remains a mysterious, somewhat confusing rulebook that they are supposed to swallow bravely, like a bitter vitamin every morning before breakfast.

Group 3 sees the Bible much differently. For them the Scriptures are alive, literally popping with exciting truths. This group doesn't live by bread alone, "but on every word that comes from the mouth of God" (Matt. 4:4).

But perhaps you're thinking that you don't quite fit in any of these three categories. If you are like a lot of Christians I have met, you land somewhere between Group 2 and Group 3. You want the Bible to be more important. You want to submit to its authority, but life sort of crowds in. Everywhere you turn you are enticed or intimidated to forget the teachings of the Scripture.

For example, you turn on a TV talk show and hear a big star make authoritative announcements such as, "I think everyone should do his own thing, live his own life and have his own faith." The studio audience bursts into applause and you are left wondering if it's really very bright (or even very American) to think that you, a born-again Christian and member of a church, have all the answers between the covers of such an old and seemingly "outdated" book.

But when we let the world's value system intimidate us, we forget a basic truth. In a world of relative thinking that has no absolutes, the Bible stands as the absolute authority for the Christian. The Scriptures are the Word of God, not man's opinions, human philosophy, somebody's ideas, not the polling of the best thoughts from the best thinkers. Scripture is God's Word and that means it has several characteristics and qualities that should make it extremely important in our lives.

GOD'S WORD IS INFALLIBLE

Some statements of faith published by churches or Christian organizations say, "The Bible is God's Word, the infallible rule of faith and practice." That is a good statement, but I prefer an even stronger one that says, "The Bible is God's *infallible* Word, the only rule of faith and practice."

There is a real difference in where you place the word "infallible" in those two statements. The second statement clearly says that *in its totality* the Bible makes no mistakes. The original autographs (the absolutely first copies) were without error. Copiers have made minor mistakes over the centuries, but none of these are serious enough to challenge the Bible's infallibility. The Bible says of itself, "The law of the Lord is perfect" (Ps. 19:7). The Bible is flawless because it was authored (inspired) by a God who is flawless.

I will discuss inspiration of Scripture in more detail in chapter 3, but the point to think about here is this: *If God is our ultimate authority and His character is flawless, and if He inspired the writers of Scripture to put down His thoughts while still allowing them freedom of personal expression, then the Bible is flawless and it becomes our ultimate authority—our only rule for faith and practice.*

To put it another way, if we believe God is perfect, then it has to follow that the original copies of Scripture—the original giving of God's Word—also had to be perfect. Is the Bible infallible? It has to be, because it is the only book that never makes a mistake.

GOD'S WORD IS INERRANT

The Bible is not only infallible in its totality but it is also inerrant in all its parts. The writer of Proverbs says it well: "Every Word of God is flawless; he is a shield to those who take refuge in him" (Prov. 30:5).

In regard to Scripture, inerrancy and infallibility go hand in hand. According to the writers of the Chicago Statement on Biblical Inerrancy, the negative terms "infallible" and "inerrant" "have special value, for they explicitly safeguard crucial positive truths." The Chicago Statement, drafted at a summit conference called in October 1978 by the International Council on Biblical Inerrancy to affirm the authority of Scripture, goes on to say:

> *Infallible* signifies the quality of neither misleading nor being misled and so safeguards in categorical terms the truth that Holy Scripture is a sure, safe, and reliable rule and guide in all matters. Similarly, *inerrant* signifies the quality of being free from all falsehood or mistake and so

safeguards the truth that Holy Scripture is entirely true and trustworthy in all its assertions.[1]

As implied in both the above definitions, one convenient way to describe infallibility and inerrancy is in the word "truthfulness." In Isaiah 65:16, the Lord calls Himself, "God of truth." In Jeremiah 10:10, the prophet writes, "The Lord is the true God." The New Testament agrees with the Old in calling God a God of truth. Examples of many such statements include: "God is truthful" (John 3:33); "that they may know you, the only true God" (John 17:3); "He is the true God" (1 John 5:20).

To make sure that we don't overlook the importance of God's truthfulness, three times the Scripture stresses that God cannot lie (see Num. 23:19; Titus 1:2; Heb. 6:18).

Some critics of Scripture, however, like to point out that biblical "truthfulness" is open to question because Scripture contains terms that are not scientifically precise or grammatically correct, and passages that seem to contradict one another. The writers of the Chicago Statement face this criticism head-on by saying:

> In determining what the God-taught writer is asserting in each passage, we must pay the most careful attention to its claims and character as a human production. In inspiration, God utilized the culture and conventions of his penman's milieu, a milieu that God controls in His sovereign providence; it is misinterpretation to imagine otherwise. So history must be treated as history, poetry as poetry, hyperbole and metaphor as hyperbole and metaphor, generalization and approximation as what they are, and so forth. Differences between literary conventions in Bible times and in ours must be observed . . .

non-chronological narration and imprecise citation were conventional and acceptable and violated no expectations in those days . . . Scripture is inerrant, not in the sense of being absolutely precise by modern standards, but in the sense of making good its claims and achieving that measure of focused truth at which its authors aimed.[2]

In a list of 20 Articles of Affirmation and Denial, the Chicago Statement further confirms the need to understand how God inspired certain men to write Scripture at certain times, under certain circumstances. Article XIII reads: "We affirm the propriety of using inerrancy as a theological term with reference to the complete truthfulness of Scripture."[3]

Testimony for the truthfulness of God is found throughout His written Word, and if we don't accept and believe that testimony, we will wind up somewhere in Group II: those who know the Bible is supposed to be important, but who remain apathetic and listless about what it says. In fact, such apathy can lead to real despair. A young man visited my office and said, "My whole Christian life is in a mess. Everything is falling apart. I can't study the Bible. I have these doubts . . ."

I listened to him for about 20 minutes and then I said, "I can tell you right now what your problem is. It's obvious."

"What is it?" he wanted to know.

I replied, "You do not believe in the absolute inerrancy of Scripture. If you believe there are errors in the Word of God, then you are confused and you don't know what to believe. That's your problem."

"You know," he said, "you hit it right on the nose. I don't believe in the absolute inerrancy of Scripture."

"Then my friend," I answered, "how can you hope to be an effective student of the Word of God or to ever lead an effective Christian life?"

Is the Bible inerrant? It has to be, because the Bible is God's Word and God is a God of truth.

GOD'S WORD IS AUTHORITATIVE

If the Bible is infallible and inerrant, it must be our final word—our highest standard of authority. The writers of the Old Testament make more than 2,000 direct claims to be speaking the very words of God. Again and again they wrote such phrases as, "The Spirit of the Lord has spoken to me" or "The Word of God came unto me." For example, Isaiah opens his prophecy by saying, "Hear, O heavens! Listen, O earth! For the Lord has spoken" (Isa. 1:2). When God speaks, everybody is to listen because He is the final authority.

In the New Testament we find more of the same, especially in the teachings of Jesus. Talking about God's Word in the Sermon on the Mount, Jesus said, "Do not think that I have come to abolish the Law or the Prophets; I have not come to abolish them but to fulfill them. I tell you the truth, until heaven and earth disappear, not the smallest letter, not the least stroke of a pen, will by any means disappear from the Law until everything is accomplished" (Matt. 5:17–18).

That even the tiniest part of God's Word has authority is echoed by James when he writes, "For whoever keeps the whole law and yet stumbles at just one point is guilty of breaking all of it" (Jas. 2:10). All of God's Word is authoritative.

But while the Bible claims complete authority over our lives, many people do not always recognize that authority. Today's "all truth is relative" way of thinking takes the Bible off its authoritative pedestal and places it on the shelf as "just another book."

In an article written for *Eternity* magazine many years ago, D. Martyn Lloyd-Jones wrote words for the church of the '50s that are even more true for the church of today. Lloyd-Jones points out that the attack on Scripture's authority began in the middle of the eighteenth century with the beginning of what came to be known as the "higher critical" view of Scripture. Naturalistic presuppositions, along with man's knowledge, new discoveries in science, and human reasoning and understanding, were all brought to bear in an attempt to analyze the Bible and "get at its real truth." All of this developed into the movement we know as liberalism, which held sway throughout the eighteenth and nineteenth centuries. Liberalism saw the Bible as full of errors, the work of men, and something to be accepted as having no more authority than the works of Shakespeare or Henry Wadsworth Longfellow.

With the dawn of the twentieth century, a new movement began. Neo-orthodox thinkers tried to restore some of the Bible's authority by reaffirming the sinfulness of man and claiming that while the Bible is not the Word of God, it "contains the Word of God." As Lloyd-Jones describes it, "The Bible, we are told, is partly the Word of God and partly the word of man. In part it has great authority and in part it has not."[4]

Lloyd-Jones goes on to point out that this "partly God's Word, partly man's word" position leads to a view of the Bible that says that part of it is of great value but there are also other parts that are full of errors and that are "utterly useless and valueless."[5] But, observes Lloyd-Jones, we are then faced with a very basic question: "Who decides what is true? Who decides what is of value? How can you discriminate and differentiate between the great facts that are true and those that are false? How can you differentiate between and separate facts from teaching? How can you separate this essential message of the Bible from the background in which it is presented? . . . The whole Bible comes to us and offers itself to us in exactly the same way. There is no hint, no suspicion of a suggestion that parts of it are important and parts are not. They all come to us in the same form."[6]

Liberalism and neo-orthodoxy are still with us in every conceivable shape and form. As Lloyd-Jones wrote in 1957, "The modern position amounts to this, that it is really man's reasons that decide. You and I come to the Bible and we have to make our decisions on the basis of certain standards, which are obviously in our minds. We decide that one portion conforms to the message, which we believe, and that another does not. We are left still with the position, in spite of all the talk about a new situation today, that man's knowledge and man's understanding are the final arbiter and the final court of appeal."[7]

From ministers and seminary students to lay people in the pews, we can all get caught up in the doubts and skepticism. Even the greatest of Christian leaders know what it is to wrestle with this. Some have wrestled and lost; others have wrestled and won.

Before he launched his career, Billy Graham wrestled with doubts about the Scriptures. Recalling those days of struggle, he says:

I believe it is not possible to understand everything in the Bible intellectually. One day some years ago I decided to accept the Scriptures by faith. There were problems I could not reason through. When I accepted the Bible as the authoritative Word of God—by faith—I found immediately that it became a flame in my hand. That flame began to melt away unbelief in the hearts of many people and to move them to decide for Christ.

The Word became a hammer, breaking up stony hearts and shaping men into the likeness of God. Did not God say, "I will make my words in thy mouth fire" (Jer. 5:14), and "Is not my word like as a fire? saith the LORD; and like a hammer *that* breaketh the rock in pieces?" (Jer. 23:29).

I found that I could take a simple outline, then put a number of Scripture quotations under each point, and God would use it mightily to cause men to make full commitment to Christ. I found that I did not have to rely upon cleverness, oratory, psychological manipulation, apt illustrations, or striking quotations from famous men. I began to rely more and more upon Scripture itself and God blessed it. I am convinced through my travels and experience that people all over the world are hungry to hear the Word of God.[8]

Is the Bible authoritative? Does it need defending? The great preacher, Charles Haddon Spurgeon, said it well: "There is no need for you to defend a lion when he's being attacked. All you need to do is open the gate and let him out."

GOD'S WORD IS EFFECTIVE

One of the most powerful claims to the Bible's infallibility, inerrancy and authority is its effectiveness. The prophet Isaiah aptly describes the ability of Scripture to get results when he said, "As the rain and the snow come down from heaven, and do not return to it without watering the earth and making it bud and flourish, so that it yields seed for the sower and bread for the eater, so is my word that goes out from my mouth: It will not return to me empty, but will accomplish what I desire and achieve the purpose for which I sent it" (Isa. 55:10–11). One of the best things about being a preacher and a teacher of God's Word is that you know it will do what it says it will do. You are not left worrying about what you will say when your product doesn't work.

There is a story about a lady who lived way out in the country. A vacuum cleaner salesman came by and began to give the woman his high-pressure sales talk.

"Madam, I have the greatest product you have ever seen. This vacuum cleaner will eat up anything. In fact, if I don't control it, it will suck up your carpet."

Before the woman could reply, he went on to say, "Lady, I want to give you a demonstration."

The salesman went to the fireplace, scooped up some ashes and threw them in the middle of the carpet. Then he reached into a bag in his own pocket and poured more dirt and junk right on the carpet. After making a thorough mess he said, "Madam, I want you to watch this product at work. I guarantee it will suck up every bit of everything I've thrown on your rug."

The woman stood there aghast—speechless—and the salesman went on to say, "Lady, if it doesn't suck up every bit of this, I'll eat it all with a spoon."

The woman looked the salesman in the eye and finally found her voice: "Well, sir, start eating. We ain't got no electricity."

It's tough to be caught in a situation where your product isn't going to work. But that never happens with the Bible. It is always effective and it always does exactly what it says it will do. Paul talked about this great effectiveness of the Scriptures when he wrote, "Our gospel came to you not simply with words, but also with power, with the Holy Spirit and with deep conviction" (1 Thess. 1:5). When the Word goes forth, it has power. It has the Holy Spirit and you have the assurance that God's Word will do what it says.

To Sum It Up

So what have we said so far? The Word of God is infallible in its totality and it is inerrant in all its parts. God's Word is authoritative and demands our obedience. Again and again we see the Bible's infallibility, inerrancy and authority demonstrated because the Bible is effective. The Bible does what it says it will do.

Everything we have said so far is good, *if* we have one more thing—the presence of the Holy Spirit. The need for this vital extra dimension is well illustrated by a conversation I had with a man on an airplane. As we talked, he continually admitted that he didn't understand the Bible. I didn't really tell him in so many words, but I hinted at why I didn't expect him to understand the Bible. He didn't have the one necessary thing he needed—the life of God in his soul by the presence of the Holy Spirit.

Without the Holy Spirit, the Bible is "just another book." When we have the Holy Spirit at work in our hearts the Bible is THE Book. We will see why in the next chapter.

SOME PERSONAL QUESTIONS

1. I know the Bible is important to me because:

2. Recently, I have looked to Scripture as the final authority in my life (my thoughts, words, behavior) in the following ways:

3. When describing the Bible, I prefer to say it is (rank in your order of preference):

_____ infallible

_____ authoritative

_____ inerrant

_____ completely true

KEY VERSES TO KEEP IN MIND

*Man does not live on bread alone, but on every word
that comes from the mouth of God.*

Matthew 4:4

*Every word of God is flawless; he is a shield to those
who take refuge in him.*

Proverbs 30:5

✿✿

CHAPTER 2

WHO CAN PROVE GOD'S
WORD IS TRUE?

✿✿

But how do we know it's true?

That question is one of the battle cries of our generation, which is also fond of asking, "Who says I have to do it?" Today it is something of a colossal understatement to say that we live in a world that doesn't respond to authority very well. In fact, just about the whole world rebels against authority. If you doubt it, ask the police. Ask teachers, coaches or congressmen. Ask employers, the Supreme Court—or the president.

Deep in the soul of every person is a streak of rugged individualism that begins in the womb and starts to show in the cradle. We all want to be our own god. We want to be captains of our soul and masters of our fate. No, we don't respond to authority very well at all.

Is it any wonder then that people question the authority of the Bible? As a minister I can say, "The Bible is the absolute authority for everyone. It is infallible, inerrant, effective, and absolutely authoritative. It is the final word on how we should all live."

The typical response—which can come from Christians as well as non-Christians—is: "Well how do I *know* that? I'm not going to accept what you say unless you *show* me."

In other words, they want proof. So what can you say when someone wants you to prove the Bible is true?

FOUR WAYS TO PROVE THE BIBLE

If I want to play the "prove the Bible is true" game, I can argue from *personal experience*. I believe the Bible is true because it gives me the experience that it claims it will give me. For example, the Bible says that God will forgive my sins. I believe that. I accepted God's forgiveness and it happened. How do I know? I have a sense of freedom from guilt.

The Bible also says that if I come to Christ, then I will be a "new creation." Old things will pass away and all things will become new. I believed in Christ one day and it happened just as the Bible said it would. Old things did pass away and all things did become new. I know, because I experienced it in my own life.

Yes, the Bible really changes lives. Millions of people— from great heads of state to brilliant educators and scientists, from philosophers and writers to generals and historians—could all testify about how the Bible has changed their lives. As somebody has said, "A Bible that is falling apart usually belongs to somebody who isn't." Millions of people are living proof that the Bible can put lives together and keep them that way.

A stronger argument comes from science. Although the Bible is not a science book, the descriptions referring to scientific processes are accurate.

Take, for example, the hydrological cycle. Rain or snow falls to the ground and runs off into streams, which run into rivers, which run into the sea. Water evaporates from the surface of the ocean and returns to the clouds, where it becomes rain and snow, which falls to the ground. The hydrological cycle is a discovery of fairly modern times, but the Bible speaks of it in Isaiah 55:10: "As the rain and the snow come down from heaven, and do not return to it without watering the earth . . ." (For similar references see Job 36:27 and Ps. 135:7.)

For another illustration, we can go to the science of geology. Geologists speak of a state called *isostasy*, which can be used to describe the balance of the earth as it orbits through space. Basically the idea behind isostasy is that equal weights are necessary to support equal weights. Land mass must be balanced equally by water mass. In order for the earth to remain stable as it spins in orbit, it must be in perfect balance. But again, the scientists haven't discovered anything that is significantly new or beyond the Bible. The prophet Isaiah also wrote that God "measured the waters in the hollow of his hand" and that He "weighed the mountains on the scales and the hills in a balance" (Isa. 40:12).

You can find many other examples of how the Bible matches up with discoveries of modern science.[1] Of course the precise technological language is not there, and for good reason. God wrote the Bible for men of all ages, and while His Word never contradicts science, it also never gets trapped into describing some precise scientific theory that becomes outdated in a few years, decades or centuries. Long before modern science was born, St. Augustine gave excellent advice to Christians when he said in effect, "We should not rush headlong to one opinion or the other, because there is always the possibility that a hastily adopted viewpoint can turn out to be false, and if our faith is dependent on that view it can appear false, too. And we will be arguing for our own opinions rather than the real doctrines of Scripture."[2]

A third significant area that has continued to prove the Bible's accuracy is archaeology. William F. Albright, recognized throughout the world as the leading Palestinian archaeologist of the twentieth century, attests that there is little doubt that archaeology has confirmed the substantial historical accuracy of Old Testament tradition.[3]

For example, higher critics of Scripture doubted the Bible's description of King Solomon's wealth. But archaeologist Henry Breasted, between 1925 and 1934, unearthed the remains of one of Solomon's "chariot cities" at Megiddo in northern Palestine. Breasted found stables capable of holding over 400 horses, also the remains of barracks for Solomon's chariot battalions, which were stationed to guard a strategic path at Megiddo. Nelson Glueck, another archaeologist, found the remains of a huge refining factory for copper and iron, two metals Solomon used when bartering for gold, silver and ivory (see 1 Kings 9:28; 10:22).[4]

Critics of Scripture also doubted the existence of the Hittites, a people the Bible refers to some 40 times. Archaeologist Hugh Winckler excavated the Hittite capital of Boghaz-Koi and recovered thousands of Hittite texts, as well as the famous Hittite code.[5]

Other examples of how archaeology confirms the authority of the Bible could fill this book and several dozen others.[6] Archaeology helps us see clearly that our Christian faith rests on facts (actual events) not myths or stories.

Perhaps the strongest objective argument for the validity of Scripture comes from fulfilled Bible prophecy. Peter W. Stoner, a scientist and mathematician, utilized what he called "the principle of probability." This principle holds that if the chance of one thing happening is one in M and the chance of another thing happening is one in N, the chance that they both shall happen is one in M × N. This equation is used in fixing insurance rates. Stoner asked 600 of his students to apply the principle of probability to the biblical prophecy of the destruction of Tyre (see Ezek. 26:3–16), which claims seven definite events:

1. Nebuchadnezzar would take the city.
2. Other nations would help fulfill the prophecy.
3. Tyre would be flattened like the top of a rock.
4. The city would become a place where fishermen spread their nets.
5. Tyre's stones and timbers would be laid in the sea.
6. Other cities would have great fear because of Tyre's fall.
7. The old city of Tyre would never be rebuilt.

Using the principle of probability in a conservative manner, the students estimated the chances of all seven events occurring as described at one in 400 million, *yet all seven did occur.* Stoner's students did a similar study on the prophecy that predicted the fall of Babylon (see Isa. 13:19). They estimated the chances of the Babylon prophecies occurring at one in 100 billion, but everything stated did come to pass.[7]

Biblical prophecy declares the events of the future with accuracy that is beyond the capability of human wisdom or anticipation. Despite astronomical odds, hundreds of biblical prophecies have come true, and they make the most objective argument for the Bible's authority.

BEYOND ARGUMENTS AND PROOFS

While there are many solid arguments for the authority of Scripture, none of them are of much use if someone doesn't want to be convinced. Martyn Lloyd-Jones, the outstanding British scholar quoted at length in chapter 1, points out: "Ultimately this question of the authority of the Scriptures is a matter of faith and not of argument . . . you may convince a man intellectually of what you're saying, but still he may not of a necessity believe in and accept the authority of the Scripture."[8]

Actually there is only one argument that can prove to us that the Bible is true and authoritative for our lives: the work of the Holy Spirit in our hearts and minds. Perhaps no one knew this better than the apostle Paul and there is no clearer description of the work in the heart of the believer in Christ than 1 Corinthians 2.

Paul opens chapter 2 by saying, "When I came to you, brothers, I did not come with eloquence or superior wisdom as I proclaimed to you the testimony about God. For I resolved to know nothing while I was with you except Jesus Christ and him crucified. I came to you in weakness and fear, and with much trembling. My message and my preaching were not with wise and persuasive words, but with a demonstration of the Spirit's power, so that your faith might not rest on men's wisdom, but on God's power" (vv. 1–5).

Paul stressed that he came to the Corinthians with nothing but the simple gospel. The gospel does not need the addition of human philosophy or wisdom. God does not need man's reason or man's innovation. Everything about the gospel is really very simple. In fact, to the world it sounds so simple it seems foolish. In 1 Corinthians 1:18, Paul writes, "For the message of the cross is foolishness to those who are perishing." And that is exactly what it was to the sophisticated Corinthians, who, like their neighbors in nearby Athens, were always seeking the new theory and the brilliant new philosophy.

In effect they said, "Paul, you're full of nonsense. Do you expect intellectuals like us, with all of our wisdom and education, to believe that somewhere, sometime one fellow died on a cross and that was the turning point of human history?" People say essentially the same thing today. "The Bible? That's for little kids and old ladies, isn't it? No intelligent person would believe the Bible. I just can't buy it." I've heard many people say things like that. And Paul agrees with them. When it comes to "human wisdom," the Bible certainly does sound like a lot of foolishness.

But Paul isn't talking about human or worldly wisdom. The only people who can know the wisdom that Paul is talking about are Christians. God's wisdom is open only to the minds of believers in Christ as Savior and Lord. Paul then goes on to make two points about true wisdom—how it is discovered and how it is revealed.

TRUE WISDOM NOT HUMANLY DISCOVERED

As I talk with people, I hear a lot of opinions about God: "Well, I think God . . ." "In my opinion, God is . . ." While we all have a right to our opinion, what we think about God can't help us a great deal as far as really getting to know Him. We can't know God on our own no matter how hard we try. We can't escape the confines of a natural existence, leap into a supernatural dimension, and then come back and tell everyone what we know about God. We don't leave this natural world. We are stuck here, unable to know God on our own.

Christians are always giving testimonies about how "I found the Lord . . ." But the Lord wasn't lost. We were, and He found us. He had to come and find us because we are not able to transcend our own natural system. That's why Paul says in 1 Corinthians 2:6 that the wisdom of this age is "coming to nothing." Paul is thinking of the philosophers who keep coming and going, arguing and changing their views. While philosophy has made contributions down through the ages, there has been a great deal of contradiction and even instability. As one philosophy professor told his class, "Philosophy bakes no bread."

Paul speaks of an entirely different kind of wisdom. He teaches "God's secret wisdom, a wisdom that has been hidden and that God destined for our glory before time began" (1 Cor. 2:7). Before time began, God had a marvelous salvation plan, and He hid it. Then, in Christ and in the New Testament all of these mysteries were revealed.

God had to reveal the mystery, of course, because the brilliant "rulers of this age" didn't understand it. If they had, then they wouldn't "have crucified the Lord of glory" (1 Cor. 2:8). The rulers of this age Paul refers to were the Jewish and Roman leaders. They didn't know God and they didn't know the truth. Again, if they had, they never would have crucified Christ. All the brilliant Romans and all those educated erudite Sadducees and Pharisees, those who were well-schooled in the Old Testament, together they all crucified Christ.

Paul then goes on to quote Isaiah and says, "No eye has seen, no ear has heard, no mind has conceived what God has prepared for those who love him" (1 Cor. 2:9). With all of the world's quests for truth, it still can't figure out what's going on. There are only two ways you can come to truth, humanly speaking. One way is objective, while the other way is subjective. One uses the external empirical experiential method, and the other method uses reason or logic. When Paul talks about "no eye has seen" or "no ear has heard," he's talking about the experiential empirical method. But God is not observable externally. We can't hear Him or see Him. He does not fit in our test tubes or under our microscopes.

The other way men draw conclusions is through their own reasoning—rationalism. And that's why Paul goes on to say that no mind has conceived what God has prepared. Worldly wisdom can't know God through the study of objective facts and it can't know Him internally through a subjective thought process. The world is in a hopeless state but God has a great plan. The secret to knowing God is loving Him through Jesus Christ. The human mind does not discover God. God revealed Himself to the human mind in Christ.

TRUE WISDOM IS REVEALED
BY THE HOLY SPIRIT

When I was a student in high school, I visited a girl in an iron lung. Fortunately, because polio has been controlled by Salk vaccine, iron lungs are not in as much use as they once were. It's terrible to see someone in an iron lung—a large casket-like affair with pumps and hoses and dials and gauges—it is not a pleasant sight. This lovely girl had to stay in that iron lung all the time. Anything that came to her had to come from the outside. She wasn't going anywhere.

In a way an iron lung is an apt illustration of the position of the natural man. Spiritually speaking, he is in an iron lung of his own capacity. If any wisdom or truth about God is going to come to him, it will have to be brought in from the outside. In his natural state, man isn't going anywhere.

And that is the point Paul is making here in 1 Corinthians 2. The Holy Spirit has invaded man's iron lung with the truth. As the Holy Spirit reveals true wisdom, three elements are discernible: revelation, inspiration and illumination.

Revelation means the disclosure of something that has previously been hidden, the unveiling of something that has been veiled. The Holy Spirit is the agent who reveals God's wisdom to the Christian as he "searches all things, even the deep things of God" (1 Cor. 2:10). No one is better qualified. As Paul points out, no one knows the thoughts of a man better than that "man's spirit within him." And "in the same way no one knows the thoughts of God except the Spirit of God" (1 Cor. 2:11).

Inspiration is the next step in the process. Inspiration is the method by which the Spirit delivers God's revelation. Paul goes on to say that we (the apostles) "speak, not in words taught us by human wisdom but in words taught by the Spirit, expressing spiritual truths in spiritual words" (1 Cor. 2:13).

Be sure to note that when Paul uses the word "we" he is not referring generally to all Christians. He is referring to the apostles and other writers of Scripture. You and I have received spiritual truth through their writings; but here Paul is talking about his own experience, how he and other apostles received spiritual truths directly from the Spirit.

Paul's reference to how the apostles have received words taught directly by the Spirit matches the teaching in John 14:26 where Jesus tells the disciples, "The Counselor, the Holy Spirit, whom the Father will send in my name, will teach you all things and will remind you of everything I have said to you." Jesus' promise is not primarily for all believers for all time. It was spoken to those who would write the New Testament. It was to many of the disciples, later to be called apostles, that God gave power to remember the words of Christ and all that He did. And how did He give that power? Through inspiration.

When Paul sat down and wrote 1 Corinthians, the Spirit of God took control of him. The Spirit of God breathed into Paul's mind what God wanted said and then Paul used his own vocabulary and his own experience to write Scripture. The Bible is not only God's Word, it is God's *words*. (For more on inspiration, see chapters 3 and 4.)

Revelation and inspiration are only two steps in the work of the Spirit as it is described here in 1 Corinthians 2. Perhaps its most important work is in the third step—*illumination*. Many people have a Bible but don't really know what's in it. Or they discover strange and interesting doctrines that are not taught by the Bible at all. The safeguard against misuse of the Bible is the illumination from the Holy Spirit. That is what Paul is talking about when he writes in 1 Corinthians 2:14, "The man without the Spirit does not accept the things that come from the Spirit of God, for they are foolishness to him, and he cannot understand them, because they are spiritually discerned."

No matter how religious he might be, the natural man can't understand the real message of Scripture. He can't get out of his iron lung. Not only that, but somebody has pulled his plug! Spiritually speaking, he is dead. In Psalm 119:18, the psalmist prays a beautiful prayer: "Open my eyes that I may see wonderful things in your law." God didn't just give us the law (the Scriptures). He also has to open the eyes of our understanding and He does this as the Holy Spirit illuminates our minds. Truth is available, but only those who are illuminated will understand it.

The natural man may be able to read God's inspired revelation, but without the illumination of the Holy Spirit it won't make sense to him. Just as a blind man can't see the sun, the natural man can't see the Son of Righteousness. Just as the deaf man can't hear sweet music, the natural man can't appreciate the sweet song of salvation. As Martin Luther said, "Man is like Lot's wife—a pillar of salt. He's like a log or a stone. He's like a lifeless statue that uses neither eyes nor mouth, neither senses nor heart, unless he is enlightened, converted and regenerated by the Holy Spirit."

"The spiritual man," on the other hand, "makes judgments about all things, but he himself is not subject to any man's judgment: 'for who has known the mind of the Lord that he may instruct Him?'" (1 Cor. 2:15–16).

This verse tells us that we have a tremendous and a heavy responsibility. The Holy Spirit is our resident teacher of truth. God's point of reference is within us, and in a spiritual sense we can be judged by no one. The world can laugh at the Christian, mock him, call him a fool and, in some places in this world yet today, kill him. But no one can judge the spiritual man (the Christian who has the Holy Spirit of Christ) because to do that means you are judging the Lord Himself.

The Christian, however, should not misuse his spiritual status. He must be careful to never think he knows it all because, obviously, there are many natural areas when he does need advice, help, correction, and even judgment. But again, in the area of the spiritual, Paul says very clearly that the Christian is judged by no man.

TO SUM IT UP

While the Christian can marshal good arguments from personal experience, science, archaeology and prophecy, he cannot finally "prove" the Bible is true and authoritative. Still, he knows the Bible is true because of his resident truth-teacher—the Holy Spirit. The Holy Spirit is the only one who can prove God's Word is true and He does this as He works in the heart and mind of the Christian whom He indwells.

SOME PERSONAL QUESTIONS

1. For me, the most convincing argument for the authority of the Scriptures is (underline):

- · My own personal experience
- · The Bible's agreement with scientific principles
- · Fulfilled prophecy
- · Archaeological discoveries

2. How does the testimony of the Holy Spirit support arguments tested in question 1?

3. The main truth I have found in God's words in 1 Corinthians 2 is:

4. If the authority of Scripture is a matter of faith and not of argument, how do I respond to a world that does not have biblical values?

KEY VERSES TO KEEP IN MIND

The man without the Spirit does not accept the things that come from the Spirit of God, for they are foolishness to him, and he cannot understand them, because they are spiritually discerned.

1 Corinthians 2:14

For the message of the cross is foolishness to those who are perishing, but to us who are being saved it is the power of God.

1 Corinthians 1:18

✦✦✦

CHAPTER 3

How Did God Inspire His Word?

✦✦✦

Have you ever watched an athlete or musician give "an inspired performance"? Have you ever heard your pastor preach what might be called "an inspired sermon"?

Most of us have heard the word "inspired" used in these ways, but frankly I question this kind of terminology. If people give inspired performances or preach inspired sermons, what is the difference between all this and what we call inspired Scripture?

Perhaps it sounds as though I am pushing a point or being picky, and perhaps I am, but for a very good reason. With the authority of Scripture under attack from every side as never before, it is important for the Christian to understand the biblical definition of "inspired." In the New Testament, the term "inspiration" is reserved solely for God's Word. The Bible was written by special men, under special conditions and the canon is closed. There are no songs, no books, no visions, no poems, no sermons that are inspired today. (For more on the canon of Scripture, see chapter 5.)

But in order to understand the difference between biblical inspiration and the rather casual way we refer to something or someone we think is "inspired" today, we need to look closely at what Scripture has to say. Inspiration is tied very closely to another term—"revelation." Revelation is God's revealing of Himself and His will. Inspiration is the way in which He did it. To reveal Himself, God used human beings who wrote the Old and New Testaments in order to set down in exact and authoritative words the message that God wanted us to receive. But first let's look at some wrong concepts of biblical inspiration.

WHAT INSPIRATION IS NOT

In order to arrive at a correct definition of biblical inspiration, we need to look at some of the erroneous concepts some people have when they talk about the inspiration of Scripture.

First of all, inspiration is not a high level of human achievement. There are people—particularly certain theologians—who say the Bible is no more inspired than Homer's *Odyssey*, Mohammed's *Koran*, Dante's *Divine Comedy* or Shakespeare's *Hamlet*. In other words, whoever put the Bible together was simply working at a high level of genius. "Oh yes," say these advocates of natural inspiration, "the Bible is full of errors and mistakes and it certainly is fallible at many points, but in regard to its ethics, its morals and its insights into humanity it reveals genius at a very high level."

This view then exalts the human authors of the Bible but denies that God really had anything to do with its authorship. God did not write the Bible, smart men did.

This is an interesting view, but it doesn't hold up. For one thing, smart men wouldn't write a book that condemned them all. Smart men wouldn't write a book that provided salvation from the outside. Smart men want to provide their own salvation; they do not want to have to trust in a perfect sacrifice made by God's Son. And one other thing: Even the smartest of men could never conceive of a personality like Jesus Christ. Even the most gifted fiction writer could not fabricate a character who would surpass any human being who ever lived in purity, love, righteousness and perfection.

Second, inspiration is not a matter of God working only through the thoughts of the writers. There are some theologians, preachers and other biblical scholars who teach thought or concept inspiration. In other words, they say that God never gave the writers of the Bible the exact words they would write. God gave them general ideas and they put these ideas down in their own words. For example, He planted the concept of love in Paul's mind and one day Paul sat down and penned 1 Corinthians 13.

The thought or concept view of inspiration claims that God suggested a general trend of revelation, but men were left free to say what they wanted and that is why (in the opinion of those who take this position) there are so many mistakes in the Bible. This view denies verbal inspiration. It denies that God inspired the very words of Scripture. The thought or concept view of inspiration has been popular with neo-orthodox theologians (who in general believe the Bible contains the Word of God but is not *the* Word of God).

But as we've already seen in 1 Corinthians 2:13, Paul made it clear that he spoke "not in *words* taught us by human wisdom but in *words* taught by the Spirit, expressing spiritual truths in spiritual *words*" (emphasis added). In John 17:8, Jesus said, "I gave them the words you gave me and they accepted them."

God communicates in words. When He sent Moses back from his wilderness hiding place to lead the Israelites out of Egypt, God did not tell Moses, "I will inspire your thoughts. I will be with your mind and tell you what to think." No, God said, "I will help you speak and will teach you what to say" (Exod. 4:12). In Matthew 24:35, Jesus said, "Heaven and earth will pass away, but my words will never pass away." God has authored the very words of the Bible. That is one reason why, in my preaching and teaching, I explain carefully the pronouns, prepositions and even small conjunctions. All of these "minimal things" often contain profound implications and spiritual truths.

We cannot have geology without rocks, or anthropology without men. We cannot have a melody without musical notes, nor can we have a divine record of God without His words. Thoughts are carried by words and God revealed His thoughts in words. The very words of Scripture are inspired. Scripture is verbal revelation.

Theologians use the term "verbal plenary inspiration" to state clearly that *all* (plenary) the *words* (verbal) of Scripture are inspired, not just some of them. And that brings us to our next point.

Third, inspiration is not the act of God on the reader of Scripture. Some theologians today teach what I call "existential inspiration." In other words, the only part of the Bible that is inspired is the part that zaps you. You read a passage and all of a sudden you get sort of an "ethical goose bump." When you get your ethical goose bump, that particular passage is inspired—to you. But, say these theologians, the entire Bible is not inspired. The writers of the Bible didn't write down God's revelation. *They wrote down a witness to God's revelation in their own lives.*

All this means that the Bible is not really authoritative. It is not the Word of God; it simply "contains the word of God." If you ask one of these theologians, "How did the Bible become inspired to you?" He will say, "Ah yes . . ." and then launch into his explanation of his "first order experience" or his " leap of faith." When you press him for exactly what he means by first order experience or leap of faith, he will say that it can't be de-fined; it is simply an existential happening.

There are still other theologians who talk about de-mythologizing the Bible. In other words, they want to get rid of the myths that they believe are in Scripture. So, they take out things like the preexistence of Christ, the virgin birth, the deity of Christ, His miracles, His substitutionary death, His resurrection, His ascension and His return and final judgment. They take all of that out and claim that, historically, none of that information is true. But they maintain that spiritually and existentially, the Bible is true if and when it sends cold shivers up and down your spine.

Now perhaps none of this makes much sense to you. It doesn't make much sense to me either. If the Bible is full of lies from beginning to end, why would I ever go to it for spiritual truth? It seems to me that if God wanted me to trust the spiritual character of the Bible, He would make sure that the historical and factual character of the Bible would substantiate its spiritual truths.

Some people refuse to believe that God performed the miracle of giving to us, through inspiration, an infallible Bible; but yet these same doubters are ready to believe that God daily performs the greater miracle of enabling them to find and see in a fallible word of man the infallible Word of God. Soren Kierkegaard—who some say was the father of the existentialist movement—wrote, "Only the truth which edifies thee is truth." I disagree completely. How can you possibly have a divinely right experience through a wrong book? If the Bible is full of lies in other areas, why am I going to believe its spiritual claims and statements? Jesus said in John 17, "Your word is truth" (v. 17). Truth is truth and something false does not become true simply because someone decides he is feeling inspired. Dr. Donald Grey Barnhouse, one of the leading Bible teachers in the twentieth century and founder of *Eternity* magazine, has put it well: "If the Bible is only the work of men, we can never lean on it for spiritual support."[1]

Fourth, the Bible is not a product of mechanical dictation. Liberal and neo-orthodox theologians like to poke fun at the conservative fundamentalist scholar and claim that he actually teaches that the Bible was dictated with some kind of mechanical method. The writers of the Bible were not writers; they were stenographers, spiritual automatons who simply cranked out what God literally dictated into their ears.

But it is obvious that's not what happened at all. The key argument against mechanical dictation is that in every book of the Bible you find the writer's personality. Every book has a different character and way of expressing itself. Every author has a different style. Yes, I suppose God could have used dictation and given us the truth that way. In fact, He really didn't have to use men. He could have simply dropped it all down on Earth in the form of golden plates (as the Mormons like to claim for the *Book of Mormon*).

I don't know why God used men, but He did. There are variations in style of biblical writing. There are variations in language and vocabulary. From author to author there are distinct personalities, and you can even feel their emotions as they pour out God's Word on paper.

Still, we have the question, How could the Bible be the words of men like Peter and Paul and at the same time be God's words as well? Part of the answer to this complex question is *simply because God had made Paul and Peter and the other writers of Scripture into the men that He wanted them to be.*

God made the writers of Scripture the men He wanted them to be by forming their very personalities. He controlled their heredity and their environments. He controlled their lives, all the while giving them freedom of choice and will, and made them into the men He wanted them to be. And when these men were exactly what He wanted them to be, He directed and controlled their free and willing choice of words so that they wrote down the very words of God.

God made them into the kind of men whom He could use to express His truth and then God literally selected the words out of their lives and their personalities, vocabularies and emotions. The words were their words, but in reality their lives had been so framed by God that they were God's words. So, it is possible to say that Paul wrote the book of Romans and to also say that God wrote it and to be right on both counts.

We have seen four incorrect views of inspiration; what is the right view? Scripture itself offers plenty of information on this question.

WHAT INSPIRATION IS

Two passages of Scripture—2 Timothy 3:16 and 2 Peter 1:20–21—tell us what inspiration really is. Many versions of 2 Timothy 3:16 say, "All Scripture is given by *inspiration* of God" (*KJV*, emphasis added). The *New International Version* of the Bible is more accurate, however, when it translates the verse, "All Scripture is God-breathed." The Greek expression used here is *pasa grafe theopneustos.* Let us take a closer look at the meaning of these three crucial words.

Theopneustos is a combination of the Greek word *theos* (God) and *pneu* (breath). We get such English words as pneumatic and pneumonia from the Greek root *pneu. Theopneustos* then literally means "God-breathed." The key to understanding the concept of "God-breathed" really comes out of the Old Testament. In Psalm 33:6, we read, "By the word of the Lord were the heavens made, their starry host by the breath of his mouth." In other words, God breathed the universe into existence. In the same way, God breathed into existence His Word, the Bible. When Scripture speaks, God speaks. Romans 3:2 tells us that the Scriptures are the oracles, "the very words" of God. When God called Samuel, Samuel answered by saying, "Speak, for your servant is listening" (1 Sam. 3:10). A few verses later we read that "the Lord was with Samuel as he grew up, and he let none of his words fall to the ground" (1 Sam. 3:19). As the first in a long line of God's prophets, Samuel made sure not to neglect a single word that God had given him.

In the first chapter of Jeremiah, that prophet writes, "The word of the Lord came to me, saying, 'Before I formed you in the womb I knew you, before you were born I set you apart; I appointed you as a prophet to the nations'" (vv. 4–5). A few verses later, Jeremiah reports, "Then the Lord reached out his hand and touched my mouth and said to me, 'Now, I have put my words in your mouth'" (v. 9). God has always worked through words, not merely thoughts. He has put His words in the mouths of the writers of Scripture.

The second point from 2 Timothy 3:16 concerns *how much* of Scripture is God-breathed. Paul uses the Greek word *pasa,* which can be translated "all" or "every." Paul is saying that all Scripture—every bit of it—is inspired.

One argument used by critics of the Bible is that 2 Timothy 3:16 can refer only to the Old Testament because that's all of the Scripture Paul had at that time. The New Testament canon was not officially approved by the organized church until sometime in the fourth century.[2] This, however, does not alter the fact of New Testament inspiration. What God inspired, He inspired (including 2 Tim. 3:16). James Packer says, "The church no more gave us the New Testament canon than Sir Isaac Newton gave us the force of gravity. God gave us gravity, by His work of creation, and similarly He gave us the New Testament canon, by inspiring the individual books that make it up."[3]

Dr. William Hendriksen adds, "Though the history of the recognition, review, and ratification of the canon was somewhat complicated . . . what should be emphasized . . . is that not because the church, upon a certain date, long ago, made an official decision (the decision of the Council of Hippo, A.D. 393; of Carthage, a.d. 397), do these books constitute the inspired Bible; on the contrary, the 66 books, by their very contents, immediately attest themselves to the hearts of all Spirit-indwelt men as being the living oracles of God."[4] The church only recognized this reality.

What does all this have to do with what Paul said in 2 Timothy 3:16? Just this: To say all Scripture is God-breathed doesn't necessarily mean just all past Scripture. I believe 2 Timothy 3:16 refers to the entire Scripture—that which had been written, that which was being written and that which was yet to be written.

As for the third point from 2 Timothy 3:16, we need to ask just what is Scripture? And here we have the other Greek word—*graphe*. This is the word from which we get graphite—the material that is used for making pencils. *Graphe* simply means "writing." Did Paul mean that all kinds of writing were inspired? Obviously not, and we can go back to 2 Timothy 3:15 to see just what he did mean. Paul tells Timothy, "From infancy you have known the holy Scriptures, which are able to make you wise for salvation through faith in Christ Jesus." So, Paul is talking about holy writing. It is the holy Scripture that is God-breathed.

Technically speaking, the writers of Scripture are never referred to as inspired. Paul is referring to their *writings* and he says that they are God-breathed. So, when we sometimes say that Paul was inspired as he wrote certain books of the Bible, this is not technically correct. Paul was not inspired. The Epistle to the Romans is inspired, as are the letters to the Corinthians, the Galatians, the Ephesians, and so on. It is not the men who wrote Scripture that are inspired; it is the message. Some writers of Scripture wrote only one brief book or letter and never wrote another "inspired" thing in their entire lives.

How Did God Guide the Biblical Writers?

What then was the condition of a biblical writer at the time he wrote inspired Scripture? What was the difference between the way Paul felt and wrote when he penned Romans and all those other letters and when he simply wrote out supply lists for his next missionary journey?

We find the answer in the other basic Scripture text that refers to Scripture being inspired or God-breathed—2 Peter

1:20–21. Here we read, "Above all, you must understand that no prophecy of Scripture came about by the prophet's own interpretation. For prophecy never had its origin in the will of man, but men spoke from God as they were carried along by the Holy Spirit." Peter is saying that no part of Scripture was of any private origin. No Scripture ever simply came out of a man's mind. There was a special condition for the writing of Scripture and Peter refers to it as being "carried along by the Holy Spirit." (Keep in mind here also that when Peter mentions "prophecy of Scripture," he is not simply referring to prophetic books. Prophecy has a much broader meaning than that—prophecy refers to forthtelling as well as foretelling or predicting the future.)

Gordon R. Lewis, professor of systematic theology at Conservative Baptist Theological Seminary of Denver, writes, "The human writers were not autonomous, but lived and moved and had their being in the all-wise Lord of All. Created with a capacity for self-transcendence in the image of God, they could receive changeless truths by revelation. Providentially prepared by God in their unique personalities they also had characteristics common to all other human beings in all times and cultures. Their teaching originated, however, not with their own wills, but God's and came to them through a variety of means. In all the human writing processes, they were supernaturally overshadowed by the Holy Spirit, not in a way analogous to mechanical or unworthy human relationships, but as one loving person effectually influences another. What stands written, therefore, in human language is not merely human, but also divine. What the human sentences teach, God teaches."[5]

To Sum It Up

Inspiration of Scripture does *not* mean: (1) a high level of human achievement; (2) God giving the writers only general thoughts or concepts; (3) God acting in some special way on the reader; (4) the writers of the Bible taking it down by mechanical dictation.

Key passages that tell us what the inspiration of Scripture does mean are 2 Timothy 3:16 and 2 Peter 1:20–21. In 2 Timothy 3:16, Paul tells us that all Scripture is God-breathed. The writings are inspired, not the writers. Peter tells us in 2 Peter 1:21 that the writers were borne along by the Holy Spirit as they wrote. No Scripture ever came only from a man's mind.

What then is "inspiration"? How did God inspire His Word? One definition is as follows: "Inspiration is God's revelation communicated to us through writers who use their own minds, their own words, and yet God had so arranged their lives and their thoughts and their vocabularies, that the words they chose out of their own minds were the very words that God determined from eternity past that they would use to write His truths."[6]

Some Personal Questions

1. After reading this chapter, I would say that the doctrine of inspiration of Scripture is (underline one):

   · Somewhat important

- Very important
- Crucial

The reason for my above choice is:

2. If the Bible does not have some special qualities that reach above and beyond "humanly inspired" works such as Shakespeare and Dante, what are the implications for my own personal faith?

3. If the Bible is inspired "only when it speaks to me," that means that the authority of the Bible is:

4. As I understand it, the difference between mechanical dictation and the writers "being borne along by the Holy Spirit" as they wrote Scripture is:

KEY VERSES TO KEEP IN MIND

All Scripture is God-breathed and is useful for teaching, rebuking, correcting and training in righteousness.

2 Timothy 3:16

For prophecy never had its origin in the will of man, but men spoke from God as they were carried along by the Holy Spirit.

2 Peter 1:21

CHAPTER 4

***

What Did Jesus Think of God's Word?

***

Can you believe in Christ but not in the authority and infallibility of the Bible? You can try, but it will leave you on the horns of a very real dilemma, and here is why: If you say you believe in Christ but doubt the Bible's truthfulness, you are being inconsistent and even irrational. Christ endorsed the Bible as true and authoritative. If you give Christ a place of honor and authority in your life, it follows that to be consistent you have to give Scripture that same honor and authority.

The Deity and Authority of Christ

Despite their lack of understanding at times, the 12 disciples definitely understood that their Master was God in human form and consequently that His word was authoritative. In response to others who decided to forsake Him, Christ asked the Twelve, "You do not want to leave too, do you?" And Simon Peter answered Him, "Lord, to whom shall we go? You have the words of eternal life. We believe and know that you are the Holy One of God" (John 6:67–69).

In the course of John the Baptist's ministry around the Jordan, certain of His followers began to have questions about this prophet: "The people were waiting expectantly and were all wondering in their hearts if John might possibly be the Christ" (Luke 3:15). John, not wishing any misconception of himself to be spread around, gave them an absolute reply: "I baptize you with water. But one more powerful than I will come, the thongs of whose sandals I am not worthy to untie. He will baptize you with the Holy Spirit and with fire. His winnowing fork is in his hand to clear his threshing floor and to gather the wheat into his barn, but he will burn up the chaff with unquenchable fire" (Luke 3:16–17).

John accurately understood his ministry both as prophet and as forerunner to Christ who would possess the authority to decide the eternal destiny of each person.

God the Father directly attests to Christ's authority through two events. One occurs at the baptism of the Lord when a voice out of heaven said of Him, "You are my Son, whom I love; with you I am well pleased" (Luke 3:22). The other is at the transfiguration where the Father speaks: "This is my Son, whom I have chosen; listen to him" (Luke 9:35).

Martyn Lloyd-Jones excellently paraphrases this latter verse: "In other words, this is the one to listen to. You are waiting for a word. You are waiting for an answer to your questions. You are seeking a solution to your problems. You have been consulting the philosophers; you have been listening; and you have been asking, 'where can we have final authority?' Here is the answer from heaven, from God: 'Hear Him.' Again, you see, marking Him out, holding Him before us as the last Word, the ultimate Authority, the One to whom we are to submit, to whom we are to listen."[1]

Jesus did not hesitate to assert His unique authority in some very definitive teachings. As part of the "I am" series, Jesus informed His listeners that He was the only bread of life (see John 6:35), the only water of life (see John 4:14; 7:37), the only light of the world (see John 8:12), the only true shepherd (see John 10:1–18), the true vine (see John 15:1–8), and the way, and the truth and the life (see John 14:6).

The Sermon on the Mount provides another illustration of the authority with which Jesus spoke. Lloyd-Jones writes, "We need to remember that it is this characteristic, personal emphasis which brings Him into contrast with the prophets. Those Old Testament prophets were mighty men. They were great personalities, entirely apart from their being used by God and anointed by the Holy Spirit. But there is not one of them who ever used this 'I.' They all say, 'Thus saith the Lord.' But the Lord Jesus Christ does not put it like that. He says, '*I* say unto you.' At once He is differentiating between Himself and all others . . . His whole emphasis is upon 'these sayings of *mine*.' Here is His claim to final authority. And if it is possible to add to such a statement, He did so when He said, 'Heaven and earth shall pass away, but *my* words shall not pass away.' There is nothing beyond that."[2]

The results were that "the crowds were amazed at his teaching, because he taught as one who had authority, and not as their teachers of the law" (Matt. 7:28–29; see also Mark 1:22; Luke 4:32). While the multitudes were accustomed to hearing their leaders substantiate their points by referring to past teachers, Jesus relied upon His own authority. The question of the hypocrites in Matthew 21:23 indicates their recognition of His authority. From where did His authority stem? Jesus freely recognized it as coming from God His Father (see Matt. 9:6,8) who gave Him complete authority: "All authority in heaven and on earth has been given to me" (Matt. 28:18).

Robert Lightner, professor at Dallas Theological Seminary, adequately summarizes the origin of Christ's authority: "The source of such authority is God, and since He was God He could speak thus. The Gospel writers make it very clear that Christ's authority was derived from God, His Father. He had been sent by the Father to do the work of the Father and to declare the words of the Father. This commission He fulfilled through the power and authority of the Father (John 17:6–8)."[3]

DID JESUS DOUBT THE OLD TESTAMENT?

What did Jesus think of the Scripture of His day, the Old Testament? Did He see it as authoritative? In Matthew 23:35, He apparently defines the Hebrew canon as the books from Genesis (Abel) to post-exilic 2 Chronicles (Zechariah), which encompass the whole Old Testament in terms of the Hebrew chronology.

It is also important to note that Jesus never quoted or alluded to any apocryphal works. Why was this so? Bible scholar F. F. Bruce explains that the Apocrypha "were not regarded as canonical by the Jews either of Palestine or of Alexandria, and that our Lord and His apostles accepted the Jewish canon and confirmed its authority by the use they made of it, whereas there is no evidence to show that they regarded the apocryphal literature (or as much of it as had appeared in their time) as similarly authoritative."[4]

Although this is admittedly an argument from silence, it is still significant that 64 times Jesus quoted or alluded to the Old Testament[5] while He never referred to other sources.

Christ put His stamp of approval on the Old Testament in several key ways.

Jesus freely acknowledged that all of Scripture pointed to Him. In John 5:39, for example, Jesus said to the Jewish leaders, "You diligently study the Scriptures because you think that by them you possess eternal life. These are the Scriptures that testify about me." Later Jesus explained to the two disciples on their way to Emmaus, "what was said in all the Scriptures concerning himself" (Luke 24:27). To the Eleven, He said, "This is what I told you while I was still with you: Everything must be fulfilled that is written about me in the Law of Moses, the Prophets and the Psalms" (Luke 24:44).

Christ also said He came to fulfill all Scripture. In Matthew 5:17, He assured the disciples that He did not intend to abolish the Law or the Prophets but rather to fulfill them. Evidence of this is that Jesus willingly submitted to the Old Testament teachings as well as correcting those who accused Him falsely (see Mark 2:23–28). Also, Jesus saw Himself as fulfilling the Old Testament prophecies.[6] In Matthew 26:24, He related that He, the Son of Man, would be betrayed "just as it is written about Him." A few verses later Jesus acknowledged to Peter that He could instantly call down 12 legions of angels to protect Himself. However, this would not have been according to God's plan: "How then would the Scriptures be fulfilled that say it must happen in this way?" (Matt. 26:54). In other words, Jesus came to fulfill Scripture. His view of Scripture was that it was all about Him and every detail had to be fulfilled.

Jesus compared the duration of Scripture to the duration of the universe. He said, "It is easier for heaven and earth to disappear than for the least stroke of a pen to drop out of the Law" (Luke

16:17). So "everything that is written by the prophets about the Son of Man will be fulfilled" (Luke 18:31).

Jesus also corroborated the historicity and validity of Old Testament people and events. For example, He confirmed the creation of Adam and Eve by asking, "Haven't you read . . . that at the beginning the Creator 'made them male and female,' and said, 'For this reason a man will leave his father and mother and be united to his wife, and the two will become one flesh'?" (Matt. 19:4–5).

Some have attempted to call the account of the first murder, in which Cain killed Abel, an allegory—fiction that teaches a spiritual truth. But Jesus, when in a confrontation with the Pharisees, said, "From the blood of Abel to the blood of Zechariah, who was killed between the altar and the sanctuary. Yes, I tell you, this generation will be held responsible for it all" (Luke 11:51).

On another occasion Jesus made reference to Lot and his wife: "But the day Lot left Sodom, fire and sulfur rained down from heaven and destroyed them all . . . Remember Lot's wife!" (Luke 17:29,32).

Another Old Testament character whom Jesus saw as historical was Daniel: "So when you see standing in the holy place 'the abomination that causes desolation,' spoken of through the prophet Daniel—let the reader understand . . ." (Matt. 24:15).

Throughout the years some have denied the historical nature of the flood. But Jesus believed in the Noahic flood. He declared, "As it was in the days of Noah, so it will be at the coming of the Son of Man. For in the days before the flood, people were eating and drinking, marrying and giving in marriage, up to the day Noah entered the ark" (Matt. 24:37–38).

And there are many other facts in the book of Genesis that He substantiated, such as the call of Moses (see Mark 12:26). In John 6:31–32, He talked about the manna from heaven. In

John 3:14, He referred to the brazen serpent lifted up in the wilderness by which Israel was healed. *Over and over again, Jesus agreed to and confirmed the authority of the Old Testament record.*

WHAT ABOUT THE THEORY OF ACCOMMODATION?

Before concluding our look at Christ's view of Scripture, we must settle one other claim made by those who challenge the authority and inerrancy of Scripture. That challenge involves the idea that perhaps Jesus made His teaching fit the beliefs current to His day. Jesus, the argument goes, accommodated His teaching so that He could communicate spiritual truths without alienating the people in Palestine, particularly the religious leaders.

According to biblical scholars Norman Geisler and William Nix, "Briefly, his theory states that Jesus, in His reference to the Old Testament, accommodates His teaching to the prejudices and erroneous views of His day. It holds that He did not actually mean that Jonah was *really* in the 'whale.' It claims that Jesus' purpose was not to question the historical truth, nor to establish critical theories, but to preach spiritual and moral values."[7]

Where, in fact, did the accommodation concept originate? John M'Clintock says that the Gnostics were the first ones to hold to this: "They asserted that Christ's doctrine could not be fully known from Scripture alone, because the writer of the New Testament condescended to the stage of culture existing at that time."[8] Later, the accommodation theory was propagated by J. S. Sember (1725–1791), the father of German rationalism, and it became a strategic part of liberalism.[9] Accommodation continues to be a favorite argument by liberal and neo-orthodox thinkers of our day who challenge the infallibility and inerrancy of Scripture, but it has several fallacies. *First, the accommodation theory allows for a subjective view of Jesus' teaching.* If any part of His words were contaminated by error, then the whole of His message is suspect. Geisler and Nix ask, "If Jesus accommodated so completely and conveniently to current ideas, how can it ever be known with certainty just what He actually believed?"[10] The obvious answer is that no one could know. We could not trust Him, because we could never be sure when He was telling the truth or when He was doing a little fast footwork for political or psychological reasons.

Second, perhaps the most serious indictment of this theory is seen in Jesus' dealings with the scribes and Pharisees. If there were any people in His day to whom He might have accommodated His teaching, it would have been these religious leaders. But Jesus repeatedly confronted the scribes and Pharisees with the literal teaching of the Old Testament.

One key example is found in Mark 7:6–13, where the traditional teaching of the scribes and Pharisees conflicted with the commandments of God. Accommodation, on the other hand, would call for Jesus to agree to their traditionalistic thinking. In Matthew 22:29, the Sadducees were the object of Christ's rebuke that they did not know the Scripture. In the following chapter, Jesus again spoke of the scribes and Pharisees who purport to be followers of Moses while in reality they hypocritically impose their traditions on others (see Matt. 23:1–4).

Third, another objection to the accommodation theory involves the character of Jesus. How could He knowingly speak untruth and yet claim to be "the truth" (John 14:6)?[11] If such is the case, His integrity is impugned and His claim to be Deity is shattered,[12] for the New Testament claims that God cannot lie (see Titus 1:2).

A fourth objection is related to Christ's use of the Old Testament.
James Packer points out that the accommodation theory "assumes that Christ's ideas about the Old Testament are unessential elements in His thought which can be jettisoned without loss to His real message or to His personal authority."[13] In fact, as we previously said, Christ was intimately connected to the Old Testament, as He pointed out to the disciples in a post-resurrection appearance: "This is what I told you while I was still with you: Everything must be fulfilled that is written about me in the Law of Moses, the Prophets and Psalms" (Luke 24:44). Earlier, on the road to Emmaus, He had explained to Cleopas and his companion "what was said in all the Scriptures concerning himself" (Luke 24:27).

The theory of accommodation must be discarded because it does not fit the evidence in the Gospel record. One cannot hold to the theory of accommodation *and* to the authority of Christ with intellectual honesty. On the other hand, to hold to His authority is to hold to the inerrancy of the Scriptures. The authority and authenticity of Christ, and the Scriptures, stand or fall together.

To Sum It Up

When examining the testimony of Jesus about the Scriptures, we have to accept one of three possibilities. The first is that there are no errors in the Old Testament, just as Jesus taught. Second, there are errors, but Jesus didn't know about them. Third, there are errors and Jesus knew about them, but He covered them up.

If the second is true—that the Old Testament contains errors of which Jesus was unaware—then it follows that Jesus was a fallible man, He obviously wasn't God and we can dismiss the whole thing. If the third alternative is true—that Jesus knew about the errors but covered them up—then He wasn't honest, He wasn't holy, He certainly wasn't God, and again, the entire structure of Christianity washes away like a sand castle at high tide.

I accept the first proposition—that Jesus viewed the Old Testament as the Word of God, authoritative and without error.

The obvious conclusion here is that Jesus accepted the Old Testament authority and passed that same authority on to the New Testament record (see John 14:26; 15:26–27; 16:12–15).[14] He saw it as the equivalent of His own word. The fulfillment record is as authoritative as the predictive record.

Psalm 119:160 tells us that "the *sum* of Thy word is truth" (*NASB*, emphasis added). That can only be true if the *parts* are truth. Based on the authority of Christ, I believe they are. *An authoritative whole demands inerrant parts.*

Reason cannot be allowed to override revelation, nor can the authority of Christ be usurped by those He created. Nothing less than the nature of God is at stake.

SOME PERSONAL QUESTIONS

1. Why is it inconsistent to say you believe in Christ and His authority for your life, but that you aren't sure of the absolute authority and truthfulness of the Bible?

2. Why is Christ's stamp of approval on the Scriptures of His day (as well as Scripture to come within the next several years) so crucial?

3. How many examples can you remember from this chapter of how Christ substantiated or verified the accuracy and historicity of the Old Testament?

4. What are the implications of the following statements:

· There are errors in the Old Testament, but Jesus didn't know about them.

· There are errors in the Old Testament, Jesus knew about them, but He covered them up.

KEY VERSES TO KEEP IN MIND

Do not think that I have come to abolish the Law or the Prophets;
I have not come to abolish them but to fulfill them.

Matthew 5:17

This is what I told you while I was still with you:
Everything must be fulfilled that is written about me in the
Law of Moses, the Prophets and the Psalms.

Luke 24:44

✳✳✳

CHAPTER 5

CAN WE ADD TO GOD'S WORD?

✳✳✳

In the last few years, the renewed interest in the Holy Spirit and use of spiritual gifts has developed an excitement and renewal in many churches. God seems to be revealing Himself and His power in wonderful ways. As we get caught up in all of this, it may be hard to see the difference between what God is saying and doing today and what He said and did in the days when Scripture was being written. Is there a difference between God's Word as given then and the word He is speaking to and through believers today? I think there is a major difference, and it's something we must keep in mind if we are to keep the authority and infallibility of the Bible in proper perspective.

WHAT DID THE WRITERS OF SCRIPTURE THINK?

Suppose you had been one of the writers of a book of the Bible. How would you have viewed your work? Would you have thought you were writing something that came out of your own mind? Or would you have thought it was coming directly from God?

A good way to get answers to these questions is to see what the writers of Scripture had to say for themselves.

As we know, there were some 40 writers of Scripture who produced the Bible over a period of 1,500 years. They lived in separate times and places and had no real opportunity for collaboration to any great degree. But there is one startling characteristic about all of them—from Moses, who wrote the first five books of the Bible, to the apostle John who concluded the New Testament canon with the book of Revelation. For want of a better term, all of these writers had an air of infallibility. Many of these men were simple people without much formal education. Yes, there were a few exceptions who would be called well-educated or sophisticated: Moses was one, Solomon was another. In the New Testament, Paul was certainly well educated as was Luke, the physician, and James.

But the rest were simple farmers, herdsmen, soldiers, fishermen, and so on. Still, all of them—educated or not—wrote with an absolute certainty that what they were writing was the Word of God. And they did it with absolutely no self-consciousness. They made no disclaimers, no apologies. They never said anything like "Now, this may sound ridiculous, but this really is the Word of God." Instead, they repeatedly and unabashedly claimed to be writing God's Word. One Bible scholar estimates that in the Old Testament alone there are over 2,600 such claims. If you want to break it down, there are 682 claims in the Pentateuch, 1,307 claims in the prophetic books, 418 claims in the historical books and 195 claims in the poetic books.[1]

A key example is Moses, who tells God at the burning bush that he cannot possibly go back to Egypt and speak up to Pharaoh to make him let the Israelites go. God replies, "Who gave man his mouth? . . . Now go; I will help you speak and will teach you what to say" (Exod. 4:11–12).

The other prophets and writers of Scripture were also certain that what they had to say was something very special. First Samuel 3 records God's visit to the boy Samuel and how He revealed His word to him. First Samuel 3:19 tells us that "the Lord was with Samuel as he grew up, and he let none of his words fall to the ground."

The prophet Isaiah opens his book by saying, "Hear, O heavens! Listen, O earth! For the Lord has spoken" (Isa. 1:2).

Jeremiah begins his prophecy by claiming, "The word of the Lord came to me" (Jer. 1:4).

In describing his commissioning by God, Ezekiel records that God told him to listen carefully and take to heart all the words that He, God, was speaking. Ezekiel was to go to his countrymen in exile and say, "This is what the Sovereign Lord says . . ." (Ezek. 3:10–11).

And no Old Testament prophet makes his calling to speak in a special way any clearer than Amos, who says he was neither a prophet nor a prophet's son, but a shepherd and a keeper of fig trees. "But the Lord took me from tending the flock and said to me, 'Go, prophesy to my people Israel'" (Amos 7:15).

And what about the New Testament writers? Did they believe as the Old Testament writers did? Did New Testament writers think they were writing the Word of God?

First of all it is interesting to see what the New Testament writers thought about the Old Testament writers. There are at least 320 direct quotes from the Old Testament in the New Testament.[2] New Testament writers refer to the Old Testament some 1,000 times in all. There can be little doubt that the New

Testament writers believed that the Old Testament was God's revelation—His inspired Word.

For example, in Romans 15:4, Paul says, "For everything that was written in the past was written to teach us, so that through endurance and the encouragement of the Scriptures we might have hope."

As he opened the book of Hebrews, the writer of that letter said, "In the past God spoke to our forefathers through the prophets at many times and in various ways, but in these last days he has spoken to us by his Son, whom he appointed heir of all things, and through whom he made the universe" (Heb. 1:1–2).

In Galatians 3:8, Paul is referring to the Old Testament when he writes, "The Scripture foresaw that God would justify the Gentiles by faith, and announced the gospel in advance to Abraham: 'All nations will be blessed through you.'"

But what do New Testament writers say about other New Testament writers? Do any New Testament writers ever claim other New Testament writers are inspired? One example is in 1 Timothy 5:18, where Paul writes, "For the Scripture says, 'Do not muzzle the ox while it is treading out the grain,' and 'The worker deserves his wages.'" The sentence about not muzzling the ox is from the Old Testament (see Deut. 25:4). But the sentence, "The worker deserves his wages," is an exact duplication of a sentence in Luke 10:7 and is found nowhere in the Old Testament. So here we have Paul referring to a New Testament book—by Luke the physician—as Scripture.

In 2 Peter 3:14–16, Peter refers to "our dear brother Paul [who] also wrote you with the wisdom that God gave him. He writes the same way in all his letters, speaking in them of these matters. His letters contain some things that are hard to understand, which ignorant and unstable people distort, *as they do the other Scriptures,* to their own destruction" (emphasis added). What is Peter saying? Two things: Paul writes in a certain way in all of his letters and what he writes is Scripture. Peter is saying that Paul's epistles are inspired—the Word of God.

Paul often claims to be communicating inspired revelation, given to Him directly from God. For example, in Galatians 1:11, "I want you to know, brothers, that the gospel I preached is not something that man made up. I did not receive it from any man, nor was I taught it; rather, I received it by revelation from Jesus Christ."

One other good example of Paul's claims to inspiration is 1 Thessalonians 2:13: "And we also thank God continually because, when you received the word of God, which you heard from us, you accepted it not as the word of men, but as it actually is, the word of God, which is at work in you who believe." Paul couldn't have said it any more plainly than that. He believed that he taught and wrote God's very word. Either Paul had a monumental ego or he was telling the truth.

Another illustration is the apostle John. In his book of Revelation, John makes many references to inspiration. For example, he concludes chapter 2 by saying, "He who has an ear, let him hear what the Spirit says to the churches" (v. 29). In Revelation 19:9, John reports that the angel told him to write, "Blessed are those who are invited to the wedding supper of the Lamb!" And then the angel added, "These are the true words of God." Revelation 21 reports that God, seated on the throne, tells him to write down all he sees, "For these words are trustworthy and true" (Rev. 21:5).

From the beginning of the Bible to the very end, its writers are fully convinced that they are speaking the true words of

God. Their work bears a mark of inspiration and authority that is unshared by any other writings before or since.

The Canon Is Closed — for Good

Coming back to the question that opened this chapter, is there a distinct difference between how God spoke long ago through prophets and apostles and how He is speaking today? Without question, God is doing some wonderful things in our own day. Through His Holy Spirit, He is in the business of guiding and empowering His children to witness, write, speak and act with extraordinary spiritual impact and power. However, He is *not* in the business of inspiring (breathing out) any more scriptural revelation. The canon is closed.

But that word, "canon," may need some definition and explaining. Mention the canon of Scripture in a group of believers and you often get puzzled looks. They know God's Word is called a two-edged sword (see Heb. 4:12) but they can't seem to recall the passage that compares it to firearms. (I suppose some people may be wondering if God's "canon" is a 12-inch or a 16-inch model!)

Actually, the word "canon" is a metaphor, a play on words. It comes from the Greek word *kanon*, meaning "a rod, or bar, a measuring rule, standard or limit."[3] This Greek term, *kanon*, originally came from a root word that meant "a reed." In Bible times a reed was used as a Hebrew unit of measure. So, the word came to mean, in a metaphorical sense, a measuring rod, or standard.

The term was used in many ways: in grammar as a rule of procedure; in chronology as a table of dates; in literature as a list of books or works that would correctly be attributed to a given author.[4] Eventually, the term "canon" was used to refer to the completed list of books given to man by God. Athanasius, bishop of Alexandria, referred to the completed New Testament in A.D. 350 as the canon.[5] In other words, he labeled the collection of 27 books used in the New Testament churches as the final part of God's revelation, which had started with the Old Testament books.

Although some of the books in the New Testament canon were challenged, the final choice of Athanasius and other Early Church fathers held up. Today, when we use the term "canon of Scripture," we are actually saying the Bible is complete. God has given us His revelation. The Bible is our standard—efficient, sufficient, infallible, inerrant and authoritative. As God's standard, it is binding and determinative in evaluating any other writing, concept or idea.

How Was the Canon Chosen?

To know what the word "canon" means is helpful, but we are still left with a key question: How did the church fathers decide which books belonged in the canon?

Although the word "canon" wasn't used to refer to the Scriptures in Old Testament times, there was still a clear concept that the Old Testament books were a unified set of sacred writings that was unique.

Two basic tests were used to determine whether a book belonged in the Old Testament canon: (1) Was it inspired by God, written by a prophet or someone with the gift of prophecy?

(2) Was it accepted, preserved and read by God's people, the Israelites?

Some writers of Old Testament Scripture were not known officially as prophets. For example, Daniel was actually a Jew who had risen to the rank of high government official while being held in captivity in Babylon. David and Solomon were two of the most famous of Hebrew kings. Ezra was a scribe. Nehemiah was the cupbearer to King Artaxerxes while in captivity in Babylon and later became governor of the restored city of Jerusalem. Still, all of these men were considered to have prophetic powers or gifts. They were used to write and speak for God.

The Old Testament canon was closed (that is, the last book was written and chosen) around 425 B.C. with the prophecy by Malachi. There was no question which books were inspired by God. In the first place, the writers claimed to be inspired (discussed earlier in this chapter), and when the people of God checked their writings, they found no errors. They fit history, geography, theology—everything they knew that would have a bearing on determining inspiration.

Jewish tradition holds that the final compilers of the Old Testament canon were part of the Great Synagogue, that school of scribes founded by Ezra after the Jews returned from captivity in Babylon. Interestingly enough, there were many attempts to add to the Scriptures back then, just as there are today. Efforts were made to add some 14 non-canonical books to the Old Testament. This collection, called the Apocrypha, included 1 and 2 Esdras, Tobit, Judith, The Rest of Esther, The Wisdom of Solomon, Ecclesiasticus, Baruch (with the epistle of Jeremiah), The Song of the Three Holy Children, The History of

Susanna, Bell and the Dragon, The Prayer of Manasses, and 1 and 2 Maccabees.

However, the Apocryphal books were not allowed into the Old Testament canon by the Jews because:

1. They were written long after the canon was completed, about 400 B.C., and lacked the prophetic quality to stamp them as inspired Scripture.[6]

2. None of the apocryphal writers claim divine inspiration, and some openly disclaim it.

3. Apocryphal books contain errors of fact and teach questionable ethics and doctrines. For example, apocryphal writings justify suicide and assassination and also teach praying for the dead.

Interestingly enough, the Roman Catholic Church accepted the Apocryphal books and they were included as part of the Roman Catholic versions of the Bible.

HOW THE NEW TESTAMENT BOOKS WERE CHOSEN

Tests used by the early Christian church to determine New Testament Scripture were somewhat the same as those used for the Old Testament books.

Was the book authored by an apostle or someone closely associated with an apostle? Again, the key question was the book's inspiration; and to be inspired it had to be written by an apostle, someone who had walked and talked with the Lord, or someone who had been a close companion of an apostle. For example,

Mark was not an apostle, but he was a close associate of Peter. Luke, the only Gentile writer of the New Testament, was not an apostle but he worked closely with Paul, who was an apostle through his special experience on the Damascus Road.

Jesus had promised the apostles the power to write inspired Scripture when He told them in the Upper Room, "But the Counselor, the Holy Spirit, whom the Father will send in my name, will teach you all things and will remind you of everything I have said to you" (John 14:26). This promise by the Lord is primarily to His apostles, not to Christians today. And the apostles knew it. As we saw earlier in the chapter, they claimed inspiration for themselves or confirmed it in the writings of their fellow apostles. Without question, the key test of Scripture was apostolic authority.

Another test applied by the Early Church was content. Did the writing square with apostolic doctrine? In those early years of the church, heretics such as the Gnostics would try to slip in a phony book, but none ever made it. If it didn't square with apostolic doctrine, it didn't pass. The doctrinal aberrations were too easy to spot.

A third test asked if the book was read and used in the churches. Did the people of God accept it, read it during worship, and make its teachings part of daily living?

And a final test determined whether the book was recognized and used by the next generations after the Early Church, especially by the apostolic fathers. Church leaders such as Polycarp, Justin Martyr, Tertullian, Origen, Eusebius, Athanasius, Jerome and Augustine used and approved the apostolic writings. It is important to note, however, that the church leaders did not force certain books on the church. No one man or group of men made a certain book canonical. God determined the canon; man discovered it through long and steady usage. The canon finally emerged through the combined conviction of church leaders, and church members working in harmony and guided by the Holy Spirit.

As with the Old Testament, a formidable group of apocryphal New Testament books also sprang up. These included the Epistle of Barnabus, the Apocalypse of Peter, the Gospel of Nicodemus and the Shepherd of Hermas. There were also "Gospels" of Andrew, Bartholomew, Thomas and Phillip. But all these failed to make the final New Testament canon because they failed one or more of the key tests of authenticity.

The canonical determination and collection of genuine and inspired books continued slowly and gradually. No church council ever decreed an "official" New Testament canon, but several councils did recognize the consensus of the people and the existence of canonical books. By the end of the fourth century, the collection was complete. The canon was closed.[7]

WHAT HAPPENS WHEN YOU ADD "MORE REVELATION"?

The false apocryphal books of the Old and New Testaments (also called the *pseudepigrapha*) were only the first attempts to add "other revelation" to Scripture.[8] Down through the centuries, and into our present day, different individuals and groups have claimed their works and writings are equal to the Bible in authority and inspiration. And always, the result has been error and spiritual chaos. For examples, you need look no further than the claims made by major cults.

The Mormons have put three such works on par with the Scripture: *Doctrine and Covenants, Pearl of Great Price* and the *Book of Mormon*. For example, the Book of Alma (5:45–46) states, "Do ye not suppose that I know of these things myself? Behold, I testify unto you that I do know that these things whereof I have spoken are true. And how do ye suppose that I know of their surety? Behold, I say unto you they are made known unto me by the Holy Spirit of God . . . and this is the spirit of revelation which is in me."[9]

The Christian Scientists have elevated *Science and Health with Key to the Scripture* to a scriptural level. One of their documents states, "because it is not a human philosophy, but a divine revelation, the divinity-based reason and logic of Christian Science necessarily separates it from all other systems."[10] Mary Baker Eddy, called "the revelator of truth for this age,"[11] wrote that "I would blush to think of *Science and Health with Key to the Scriptures* as I have were it of human origin and were I apart from God its author. I was only a scribe."[12]

The Jehovah's Witnesses commit the same error when they say of their publication, "*The Watchtower* is a magazine without equal on earth, because God is the author."[13]

Another classic illustration of someone thinking he has new revelation is David Berg, leader of the Children of God. Also referring to himself as Moses, a latter-day prophet, and David, King of Israel, Berg wrote some 500 letters in five years. According to a report in *Christianity Today*, "Berg, who is said to have several concubines, insists that his letters are 'God's Word for today' and have supplanted the biblical Scriptures (God's Word for yesterday)."[14]

The preceding are only a few examples, but they illustrate a vital point that is as true today as it was when the canon was being chosen: Whoever criticizes, questions, challenges, subtracts from or adds to the authoritative Word of God is ultimately undermining the divine authority of the Lord Jesus Christ and putting man, the creature, in a place of authority instead.

TO SUM IT UP

The writers of Scripture spoke with special conviction and authority that could come only from God. They did not use phrases like "I think I am right" or "You probably won't agree with me, but . . ." Instead they said again and again in different ways, "Thus saith the Lord" and "God has put His words in my mouth." They did not guess their writings were inspired; they *knew* it.

The "canon of Scripture" is a term all Christians should know and understand better. It includes the 66 books that have been determined to be the infallible rule of faith and practice for the church for all time. Since the close of the New Testament canon in the fourth century, some people have wondered if we shouldn't be able to add to the canon. After all, God has continued to act and speak since those first centuries through the Holy Spirit of Christ. But Revelation 22:18 clearly states, "I warn everyone who hears the words of the prophecy of this book: If anyone adds anything to them, God will add to him the plagues described in this book." Of course you can scoff and say this warning applies only to the book of Revelation, not the entire Bible. But before you congratulate yourself too loudly, realize that the book of Revelation is the last book of the Bible, by its very nature, by its content and by choice of those who determined the canon. If you add to Revelation, you add to the Bible and put yourself in danger of the curse in Revelation 22:18.

Admittedly, literal plagues have not necessarily come upon some of those who have added to Scripture. (In other cases, their fates have been sad and even terrible.) God may be withholding the force of the curse in Revelation 22:18 until Judgment day. But one thing is clear: To allow anyone or everyone to claim to be speaking revelation from God is to pay too high a price. Christ has put His own stamp of authority on Scripture. The church has discovered the canon of God's Word under the guidance of the Holy Spirit. To abandon, or even downplay in the slightest way, the uniqueness of Scripture as the only truly inspired Word of God is to invite a spiritual free-for-all.

SOME PERSONAL QUESTIONS

1. How important is it to you that the writers of Scripture claim with absolute certainty to be writing the Word of God? Suppose no writer of Scripture had made any such claim. Would it make any difference in how you view the Bible's authority for your own life? Why or why not?

2. Has the choice of the scriptural canon ever been a problem for you? Among the tests for canonicity applied to the Old and New Testaments, which ones are the most important to you, and why?

3. The final sentence of this chapter states: "To abandon, or even downplay in the slightest way, the uniqueness of Scripture as the only truly inspired Word of God is to invite a spiritual free-for-all." Do you agree or disagree? Why?

KEY VERSES TO KEEP IN MIND

In the past God spoke to our forefathers through the prophets at many times and in various ways, but in these last days he has spoken to us by his Son, whom he appointed heir of all things, and through whom he made the universe.

Hebrews 1:1–2

I warn everyone who hears the words of the prophecy of this book: If anyone adds anything to them, God will add to him the plagues described in this book.

Revelation 22:18

PART II

✱✱

WHAT DOES GOD'S
WORD DO FOR US?

We have all heard that the Bible is good for us—that we should read it daily and study it often. But just why is it good for us? What does Scripture actually *do*? The next five chapters will deal with some of the basic benefits of Bible reading and study:

- *God's Word: Source of Truth and Freedom.* Is there a difference between having knowledge and having truth? What does having truth have to do with being free? How free are you?

- *God's Word: Guide to His Will.* Can the Christian actually know God's will for his or her life? Do we have to find God's will, or is it already in plain sight? What does Scripture say?

- *God's Word: The Way to Grow.* Why don't all Christians grow at the same pace? How important is the Bible to spiritual growth? How fast are you growing right now?

- *God's Word: The Perfect Pruning Knife.* What does it mean to bear Christian fruit? How much fruit are you bearing? Where does God's Word fit in?

- *God's Word: The Ultimate Weapon.* How well can you use the sword of the Spirit? Can you wield it deftly to parry Satan's attacks? Can you take the offensive against the world, the flesh and the devil?

Some of these may sound too simple, but don't let the labels fool you. Each one is a powerful element for Christian living.

CHAPTER 6

****

GOD'S WORD: SOURCE OF TRUTH AND FREEDOM

****

What is truth?

Pilate asked Jesus that question and people are still asking Him the same question today. As I talk with this person or that about the truth to be found in Jesus Christ, they reply, "Well, I don't quite know what the truth is." Some even claim to have stopped looking. One man told me, "I used to hassle myself about whether or not I'd really ever know everything and get it all figured out, and I just finally decided to set it aside and forget it. I don't need that grief. So I just don't bother to worry about it."

Granted, "knowing *everything*" and "getting it *all* figured out" is enough to discourage anyone. No doubt about it, we have a lot of information, a lot of knowledge, but we are still not sure about the truth. The Bible mentions people who are "ever learning, and never able to come to the knowledge of the truth" (2 Tim. 3:7, *KJV*).

For a lot of people, life is like that. They read and study and think and talk and listen, but they never find the truth. They never settle on anything and the frustration is overwhelming.

While at a Bible conference, I took time out for a walk. As I got away from the campground, I came upon a young fellow living in a pup tent. It turned out that he was a graduate of Boston University who had simply dropped out of society and gone on drugs. He seemed completely spaced out.

"What are you doing?" I asked.

"I searched for the answer so long and never found it," he said. "I finally decided to blow my mind on drugs and now at least I don't have to ask any questions."

Another time I was talking to a group of about 10 young people who had dropped out to live in a woodsy campsite commune. They started giving me their philosophy of life, so I asked the ultimate question: "What is truth?" They all looked at each other, almost stunned. Then a fellow stepped out of the group and said, "Yin Yang."

"Yin Yang?"

"Yeah, man, Yin Yang is where it's at."

"What's Yin Yang?" I wanted to know.

"You don't know what Yin Yang is? How can you live without Yin Yang? Here, I'll show you."

So he took a stick and drew an oblong circle on the ground. Then he drew a curved line through the middle of the oblong circle and made two equal parts. Next he drew two circles of equal size in each part of the original oblong circle. This gave him two sets or opposites. Then he said: "See it? That's Yin Yang, man. Groove on that."

"What does it do?" I wanted to know.

"Don't you get it?" he said. "Don't you know that if there wasn't black, there wouldn't be a white? If there wasn't an up, there wouldn't be a down? If there wasn't an out, you wouldn't understand what an in was?"

After he went through a string of opposites, I asked, "So what does that do for me?"

"That's where it's at, man. That's Yin Yang. Life is opposites."

I said, "You mean you've lived all your life and only discovered Yin Yang, and that's it?" All he had to hang on to was Yin Yang. The only truth he had found was the elemental concept of opposites!

My commune friend may be an extreme example, but he illustrates the plight of a lot of people. Their souls long for truth, but they remain in the chains of doubt, indecision, never quite knowing—or Yin Yang.

WHAT GOD'S WORD SAYS ABOUT TRUTH AND FREEDOM

The best place to go to find just where and how the Bible is the source of truth and freedom is to the words of Truth Himself: Jesus Christ. In the eighth chapter of John, Jesus is in one of several hot arguments with Jews who are challenging His teachings. Some of these people, however, are beginning to believe, at least a little bit, and "even as he spoke, many put their faith in him" (John 8:30). All this sounds encouraging until we take a closer look. Most biblical commentators believe that at this point these people might be called "half converts." Their faith is not enough to set them free from sin, not enough to save them.[1]

They are beginning to believe that Jesus is who He claims to be: the Messiah. Jesus wants to take them from their half-faith to full faith and full salvation. He wants to take them all the way to real truth and real liberty, and in the next few verses we can hear Him talk about three concepts: the progress of freedom, the pretense of freedom and the promise of freedom.

THE PROGRESS OF FREEDOM

How does anyone make progress toward real freedom? In John 8:31–32, Jesus spells it out: "To the Jews who had believed him, Jesus said, 'If you hold to my teaching, you are really my disciples. Then you will know the truth, and the truth will set you free.'" This is how to progress toward freedom. First you believe, then you hold tight to Christ's teaching. Holding on to His teaching—"continuing in His Word" as other versions have it—is evidence of true faith.

Why did Jesus say this to the crowd? Because He recognized their condition of half-faith. The same thing had happened back in the second chapter of John. Jesus had just finished cleansing the Temple of money changers and John observes that "many people saw the miraculous signs he was doing and believed in his name" (John 2:23). Did Jesus celebrate or say "Amen"? Hardly. "But Jesus would not entrust himself to them, for he knew all men . . . he knew what was in man" (John 2:24–25).

Jesus knew that their faith was not saving faith. They believed what they had seen Him do, but there was no commitment.

You can find the same problem in several other scenes in Scripture. When Jesus teaches the parable of the sower, He talks about seed falling on rocky soil. This represents people who believe but have no real root, no commitment. When temptation or trial comes, they fall away (see Luke 8:11–15). In John 12:42–44, you can read about Jewish leaders who believed in Jesus, "but because of the Pharisees they would not confess their faith for fear they would be put out of the synagogue; for they loved praise from men more than praise from God." They believed, but they would not confess. They were caught in the middle, believing partially but not completely—in a state of half-faith.

The point of all these examples is that "believing" in Christ is not enough. James tells us that "even the demons believe . . . and shudder" (Jas. 2:19). I have talked to a certain man for years about Christ and salvation. His answer? "I believe everything, but I am not ready to give Him my life." That says it all. There must be belief, but there must also be confession—commitment.

And that is why Jesus tells this crowd of Jews, "If you continue in My word, then you are My disciples indeed" (John 8:31, *NKJV*). James tells us, "Faith without works is dead" (Jas. 2:17). Jesus is saying the same thing. He is saying, "Show me the character of your faith by continuing in my Word—by doing what I say and living as I live." The word "continue" implies obedience. The true disciple *continues*, *abides* and *obeys* the living Word of the living Christ.

Many Christians make a false dichotomy out of receiving Jesus as Savior and Lord. They will say, "Three years ago I accepted Christ as Savior, but tonight I want to make Him Lord." Their motive for making such a statement is excellent, but they are a bit mistaken. We don't *make* Christ Lord; He already *is*. When you receive Him as Savior, He becomes Lord as well. The question is not, "Is Christ Lord of my life?" The question is, "Do I obey Christ's Lordship?"

There are people who claim to be Christ's disciples, but they have little love for His Word, for the truth. A true disciple is oriented to the Word of God. People say to me, "Why do you just teach the Bible?" What else am I supposed to do? Where else are Christians to find and learn the truth?

The word "disciple" means, literally, a learner. A true disciple loves to learn at the feet of Jesus. And then he or she gets up, goes out and gets involved. A true disciple is not just a hearer, but a doer as well (see Jas. 1:22). When we sit at the feet of Jesus, we shall *know* the truth and we shall be able to *do* the truth. Why? *Because He is the truth.*

But there is even more. In John 14:26, Jesus tells His disciples, "But the Counselor, the Holy Spirit, whom the Father will send in my name, will teach you all things." True, this promise was primarily for the disciples themselves. As we saw earlier, the Holy Spirit did come to guide and empower them as they wrote inspired Scripture. But Jesus' promise of the Holy Spirit extends to every believer in every age. God plants the Holy Spirit in your life and then He guides you into more and more truth.

But that's not all. God also provides the textbook for learning truth. In John 17:17, Jesus prayed for His disciples and said, "Sanctify them by the truth; your word is truth." And where is God's Word? In the Scriptures.

So we have Christ, Truth incarnate. We have the Holy Spirit, our Counselor and Guide (not a drill sergeant). And we have the textbook, the Bible, God's inspired infallible Word. It all adds up to the truth and once we discover the truth, says Jesus in John 8:32, we are free. Free from what? Free from the chains of spiritual death; free from the prison of sin; free from Satan's binding power; free from the search for truth; free from the frustrations of having to settle for nihilism, dropping out, or Yin Yang.

THE PRETENSE OF FREEDOM

Coming back to the scene in John 8, we note that the Jews listening to Jesus don't respond too positively. Instead of accepting His offer, they build a wall of self-righteousness. In John 8:33, we hear them saying that they are descendants of none other than Abraham. They have never been slaves to anyone. How can Jesus say that they shall be set free? Who needs it? As for never being slaves, these people seem to have short memories. At the moment they are in bondage to Rome. Before that it was the Syrians and the Greeks. Before that it was the Babylonians and before that it was the Egyptians. Every time they celebrated the Passover, they were remembering release from a time of slavery.

But let's give them the benefit of the doubt and assume they are not talking about political freedom, but instead the freedom of their spirits, their souls. Perhaps they are saying, "In our hearts we are free because we are God's chosen ones." Here they are on ground that is a little better, but still very shaky. They are trying to get to heaven on Abraham's coattails. They think God will accept and bless them because of their racial descent. They are so sure they are saved through Abraham that they throw up a wall Jesus can't penetrate. He offers them freedom, but they don't need it, or Him.

These stubborn Jews illustrate perfectly a basic scriptural principle. You can't give someone a drink unless there is thirst;

you can't give someone food unless there is hunger; you can't give someone freedom unless there is an awareness of slavery. But Jesus doesn't give up. He gets right to the point: "I tell you the truth, everyone who sins is a slave to sin" (John 8:34). Jesus cuts right through their hypocrisy and sham. He confronts the Jews with their sin, and they all know they have plenty of that. In fact, right here John uses the Greek word *doulos*, which means "bond slave"—someone in the most base kind of slavery. Jesus says, in effect, "You think you are free, but you are the most slavish of the slaves."

THE PROMISE OF FREEDOM

But Jesus doesn't leave His Jewish listeners in bondage. First, He gives them a warning by saying, "Now a slave has no permanent place in the family, but a son belongs to it forever" (John 8:35). In the newer translations the word "son" has a small *s*, which is correct. Jesus isn't referring to Himself, but to sons in general who have permanent rights in their homes, while slaves have none. Slaves can be cast out at any time.

Why tell these Jews this? Because the Old Testament era was ending. Their Abrahamic security had faded. Unbelieving Jews were just as condemned to spiritual slavery as unbelieving Gentiles. So, what can they do? How do they become sons, not slaves? Jesus goes right on: "If the Son sets you free, you will be free indeed" (John 8:36).

The only one who can free a slave is someone with rightful heirship or place in the family. Only the father or the son can release the slaves. The same is true on a spiritual plane. If Christ the Son sets you free, you are free indeed. Whoever believes in and continues to follow the Son is a son of God himself (see John 1:12).

In a few brief sentences, Jesus offers the crowd of hostile Jews real truth and real freedom. Do they accept? You can read about the outcome in the rest of John 8, but Jesus says it all in verse 37. They—the Jews—are Abraham's descendants. They have a wonderful heritage of God's guidance, truth and faith, but Jesus observes, "Yet you are ready to kill me, because you have no room for my word." Before the scene is played out, the crowd picks up stones to stone Jesus, but He slips away. They turn from the truth and choose slavery rather than freedom.

How Free Am I?

About now you may be saying, "All this is interesting, but I'm a bit farther down the road than that. I have admitted my need. I am no slave of sin. I'm a son of God and know it. Can the Bible be a further source of truth and freedom for me, or do I already have all it has to offer?"

Or perhaps you are having a few gnawing doubts. It says right there in John 8 that the Son shall make you free indeed, but you don't always feel that free. Why not? The answer is back in John 8:31: *If you hold to Christ's teaching* you are really His disciple. If you continue in His Word, you are a true learner at His feet, and He has a great deal to teach you.

Throughout history every generation has probably thought it was living in the most challenging, difficult time that could be experienced. We are no exception and we have good reason to be concerned. Technology is running amuck. We have the finest, the best, the greatest, the biggest and the most, but we are in big trouble. The miracle of the motion picture produced porn flicks. The miracle of TV brought a growing flood of subtle (and not so subtle) filth, relative morality or no morality at all into our living rooms. And you can bet your Nielsen ratings it will get worse. The miracle of the split atom has unfortunately blessed mankind with Hiroshima, Nagasaki and the constant threat of world devastation. Now the advent of the Internet, despite putting incredible amounts of useful information at our fingertips, produced new avenues for more pornography and more filth to enter our homes and lives.

The list could go on but the point is obvious: Technology and education can be wonderful things but they can also be a curse. Technology is not truth. In fact, we need the truth to help us control our technology! Truth is more than technology or information or knowledge. Truth is more than facts. Modern man is the best user of facts in history, but he lacks truth: the understanding of the meaning of things, the perception of how things really are and what to do about it.

But Jesus says we can know the truth and His truth can set us free. He has given us His truth in His Word. The next important step is ours. If we say, "Yes, Lord, I believe you have the truth," but we fail to learn that truth, we remain bound by our own ignorance and chained by our own frustration. How much of God's truth is really yours? Do you know where to go in the Scriptures to find the truth about God or about man or about life or about death?[2] Could you quickly locate passages that tell you His truth about relationships between men and women, husbands and wives, parents and children, or friends and enemies?[3] The Bible even gives us the truth about what to eat and drink, how to live and how to think. Do you know where it talks about these principles?[4]

In the Scriptures we can find what is right and what is wrong. We can know what really matters, what is truly meaningful and purposeful. We can learn where and how to commit our lives and know that we can count on the results. In Christ we can know the truth, continue in the truth and be free indeed!

To Sum It Up

Jesus promises that we shall know the truth and the truth shall set us free. We gain access to His truth by believing in Him and then *holding to His teaching*. The challenge for every disciple is this: "How much of the Scripture—the truth—is really mine? Am I holding to Christ's Word, or am I drifting in the twilight zone, toward the marshy ground of half-faith?"

To say that you believe the Bible is not enough. The devils believe and tremble. Some of us say that we believe and don't even twitch a little. But we ought to.

Christians don't claim to "have everything all figured out." They don't need to. They have the truth in Christ and His Word. Christians continue to hold to the Word—the teachings of their Lord. He is the truth.

Some Personal Questions

1. In this chapter a Boston University graduate says he dropped out and went on drugs and now at least he

doesn't "have to ask any questions." Is "not having to ask any questions" a good state to be in? Why or why not?

2. If "continuing in Christ's word" and "holding fast to His teachings" is the sign of a true disciple, how do you rate yourself on a scale of 1 to 10, with 10 being "truly faithful"?

3. The Scriptures say knowing Christ makes you free indeed. How can you tell you are free? What still seems to bind you in some way?

4. What is the difference between "having things all figured out" and having the truth in Christ and His Word?

KEY VERSES TO KEEP IN MIND

If you hold to my teaching, you are really my disciples. Then you will know the truth, and the truth will set you free.

John 8:31–32

If the Son sets you free, you will be free indeed.

John 8:36

CHAPTER 7

GOD'S WORD:
GUIDE TO HIS WILL

Whenever I get into a spiritual discussion with anyone, sooner or later we seem to get around to what God wants in a given situation. How to know God's will, how to find God's will (and sometimes how to avoid God's will) are major concerns for most Christian believers.

Along with the concerns, I often detect quite a bit of confusion. People say, "I do this because it's God's will"; and other people say, "I don't do that very same thing, because it's God's will." I heard of one fellow who advised putting all the arguments for doing something in one column and all the arguments against it in the other column. Whichever column came out the longest was the way to go! You don't have to read the daily papers very long until you see that God's will—or what people think is God's will—gets blamed for much bizarre and even tragic behavior.

Then a lot of people I talk with seem to think that God's will has been misplaced. They keep telling me, "I'm searching for God's will." Whenever I hear that, I ask, "Is it lost?" The concept of searching for God's will makes it seem as though

God might be the big Easter bunny in the sky. He hops around the universe stashing His will under some supernatural bush while we run through life trying to find it. Every now and then He calls down, "You're getting warmer!"

Still other people see God as sort of a cosmic killjoy, always making people do something miserable or boring. Then there is also the casual catch-the-brass-ring-on-the-merry-go-round-of-life approach, which says, "If you find the will of God, that's great, but if you don't, there's nothing to worry about. You're still going to heaven."

With all these concepts and misconceptions, what *is* God's will? Can we actually know? Can we pin it down? Does God really have a will for your life and mine? I believe He does and that He hasn't hidden it anywhere. If God has a will, He will reveal it.

There are any number of formulas and systems dealing with how God reveals His will. Some of them are excellent, such as *Getting to Know the Will of God*, by Alan Redpath. He compares finding God's will to sailing a ship according to three navigation lights: the Bible, the inward witness of the Holy Spirit, and outward circumstances. When all three lights are in line with one another, it is all right to proceed.[1]

Psychologist James Dobson offers four criteria for testing your impressions and leadings to see if they are God's will: (1) Is it scriptural? (2) Is it right? (3) Is it providential? (4) Is it reasonable?[2]

In his helpful book, *Living God's Will*, Dwight L. Carlson lists at least 10 specific steps for knowing the will of God: being obedient, being open, using God's Word, prayer, the Holy Spirit, counsel from others, providential circumstances, evaluation, deciding, and having peace.[3]

Interestingly enough, all three of the systems I've mentioned talk about using Scripture. Some years ago I decided to do my own study to determine that the will of God is for believers, *according to His own Word*. The formulas were useful, but I kept wondering, *What does the Bible actually say about "God's will"?*

So I went to the Scriptures and studied every passage I could find on God's will. I discovered five basic principles every Christian can use to know God's will for his or her life.

PRINCIPLE #1: SALVATION IS FOR EVERYONE

Primary among those things that God wills, according to His Word, is this promise from 2 Peter: "The Lord . . . is long-suffering . . . not willing that any should perish, but that all should come to repentance" (2 Pet. 3:9, *KJV*). You find that same thought in 1 Timothy, where Paul says that God "will have all men to be saved, and to come unto the knowledge of the truth" (1 Tim. 2:4, *KJV*).

Actually, salvation is where the will of God begins for all of us. Jesus makes this very clear in a brief passage in Mark. His mother and brothers arrive where He is teaching and begin asking for Him. The crowd tells Him, "Your mother and brothers are outside looking for you" (Mark 3:32). Jesus replies, "Who are my mother and my brothers?" (Mark 3:33). Then, looking at those seated around Him listening to His Word, He answers His own question: "Here are my mother and my brothers! Whoever does God's will is my brother and sister and mother!" (Mark 3:34).

What Jesus was saying was this: "The will of God is that you be related to me through faith, not through human family ties."

How willing was God that we be saved? "Because of his great love for us, God, who is rich in mercy, made us alive with Christ even when we were dead in transgressions—it is by [His] grace you have been saved" (Eph. 2:4). God was so willing for all to be saved that He sent His own Son to die, to make His will possible.

Unfortunately, telling people that it's God's will that they be saved isn't always popular. I can recall when I took part in an evangelism "blitz" by Campus Crusade for Christ on the campus of UCLA. We made quite a stir by witnessing to everyone and anyone we could find. The next day, the *Daily Bruin*, the campus newspaper, carried a major story and a cartoon showing the Bruin mascot lying on the ground with a Christian's heel in his neck, as if the Christian had slain the poor little bear. The Christian was labeled CCC in a fashion that unmistakably reminded us of KKK—Ku Klux Klan.

Included in the article was a quote by the dean who said that there would be disciplinary action if the blitz was not stopped immediately. He also quoted from the university charter, which said the campus "was not to be used for religious conversion." We stopped, of course, but we found it all a bit ironic. Students can attend UCLA and come out atheists, agnostics or psychological basket cases because they feel totally alienated from God and their fellowman, but "getting saved" is against the rules. You have to go across the street to do that.

Why is getting saved so unpopular on a secular campus? Because getting saved deals with sin and secular man does not want to respond to any message that talks about his sin. But this is where it all starts. Until you know Jesus Christ personally, you have never taken step 1 into the will of God.

PRINCIPLE #2: BE SPIRIT-FILLED

According to God's Word, a second step toward God's will is to be Spirit-filled. In the fifth chapter of his letter designed to help the Ephesian Christians resist slipping back into legalism, Paul says, "Be very careful, then, how you live—not as unwise but as wise, making the most of every opportunity, because the days are evil. Therefore do not be foolish, but understand what the Lord's will is. Do not get drunk on wine, which leads to debauchery. Instead, be filled with the Spirit" (Eph. 5:15–18).

I used to wonder why Paul would contrast being filled with the Spirit with getting drunk. Somehow, it didn't seem appropriate. But then I finally got the point. When you get drunk you submit yourself to the control of alcohol, which permeates your system. And when the alcohol takes over, you become the kind of person alcohol influences you to be. That's what "under the influence" means. And it is also clear that the pagans of Paul's day believed drunkenness enhanced their communion with their gods. Paul shows that it is not wine that does that, but the Holy Spirit. He opens us up to God.

I had a friend who was an alcoholic. From the time he was 17 until he was 22 I doubt he was sober more than two weeks at a time. While sober he was quiet, meek and mild. When intoxicated he turned into something else. One night he called me, raving drunk, so I went over to try to help him. When I walked in he picked up a bottle of Jack Daniels and sailed it across the room right at me. I ducked and it splattered all over the wall. I decided to leave and come back later when he was a little less under the influence of "old Jack" and his friends.

Paul uses the graphic negative example of being drunk to illustrate what it means to be filled with the Spirit. When you yield control of yourself to alcohol, it takes over. And when you are Spirit-filled, obviously the Spirit takes over. In both cases "self-control" is gone and replaced by something or someone else. In both cases there is total yielding to a power within. And the amazing thing about being under control of the Spirit is that you don't even have to ask questions, you just operate within the will of God.

One way to get a practical handle on the Spirit-filled life is to see it as living every single moment in the conscious presence of Jesus Christ. The Spirit-filled life is no great mystery; it is simply Christ-consciousness.

One note of caution, however: To be Christ-conscious does not mean walking around muttering, "I know You're there . . . I know You're there . . . I know You're there . . ." That's the legalistic, fetish approach that was used by the Pharisees. They were sometimes called "the bruised and bleeding Pharisees," a name they picked up because they thought it was a sin to look upon a woman. Every time a woman came along, they closed their eyes, muttered something about "I can't look . . . I can't look . . ." and walked smack into a wall or a tree!

No, being Spirit-filled is a matter of living every day, with your eyes wide open, saturated with the presence of Christ. And how do you get saturated? By studying His Word. The more I focus on Christ in the Word of God, the more the thoughts of God saturate my mind; and the more God's thoughts saturate my mind, the more yielded I am to Him.

Unfortunately, when it comes to God's will a lot of Christians skip this crucial step of being Spirit-filled. Instead they jump right over to wondering if they should marry Suzy or George, should they go to this school, take that job, buy that kind of car, etc., etc., etc. They pray and pray for God's will and they still haven't yielded control to the Holy Spirit. No, God's will is not lost or hidden. It's there in plain sight in His Word—be saved, then Spirit-filled!

PRINCIPLE #3: BE SANCTIFIED

A third clear teaching in God's Word about His will concerns our sanctification, or in simpler and more useful terms, our purity and holiness. While writing to the Christians at Thessalonica, Paul said, "It is God's will that you should be holy; that you should avoid sexual immorality; that each of you should learn to control his own body in a way that is holy and honorable, not in passionate lust like the heathen, who do not know God" (1 Thess. 4:3–5).

"Purity" and "holiness" are often uncomfortable terms for Christians. They sound so self-righteous and sanctimonious. Actually, purity and holiness are two crucial parts of practical Christian living.

In 1 Thessalonians 4:3–4, you can find several principles for purity. The first one is plain enough: "Avoid sexual immorality." Stay away from sexual sins. Did Paul mean sex was evil? Of course not. Sex is a beautiful, glorious human relationship—within marriage. But sexual immorality ("fornication" in some versions) refers to sexual sin outside the marriage bond, everything from premarital sex to perversions like bisexuality and homosexuality.

There is a tendency, of course, on the part of older adults to relegate most sexual sins to the young. Adults in their 30s on up cluck concernedly over the escapades of the teenagers and couples in their 20s who are living together without benefit of marriage.

But sexual temptations and living-together arrangements are not the exclusive possession of youth. In fact, there may be *more* problems among those in their 30s, 40s and 50s. The struggles of men in mid-life crisis have been well documented by Jim Conway.[4] And, of course, the women are having their problems, too. As one wife put it, "All of a sudden . . . I've noticed the streets are full of men . . . For years I must've been going by them with my eyes closed, but now I see them all right. I hardly see anything else."[5]

No matter what your age, the sex drive is a powerful force. If the Holy Spirit is not in control, it is too easy to go over the line. Where is the line? When you have to start asking that, you've probably gone over it already.

Another principle for purity in 1 Thessalonians 4:3 simply adds that *each of us* should control his (or her) own body. There are no exceptions, no special privileges. There are people, you know, who don't engage directly in immorality, but they entertain themselves by watching others who do. I recall hearing a group of students at a Christian college who decided to use their Christian liberty to watch a porn film. Of course they made a lot of excuses about how *they* would never do what they were watching. But if you go out and watch it, you may as well have done it as far as its effect on your purity is concerned.

Keep in mind, also, that while you may be able to say you have never seen this kind of film, you may be watching the same thing in principle right in your living room. Television becomes more loaded with violence, soft porn and other trash with each new season. What are *you* watching?

Today, evil, lust and immorality come in all kinds of wrappings. God's will, according to 1 Thessalonians 4:3-4, is that no Christian be entertained, interested or enticed by it. Christian purity and holiness is not sanctimonious, self-righteous drivel. It concerns right where we live daily and is a crucial part of doing God's will. If we are running around trying to find God's specific answers for certain questions but are living impure lives, why should God give us those answers when we still haven't obeyed a major part of His will that He has already revealed?

God's will is that we be saved, Spirit-filled and sanctified—set apart as pure and holy people fit for His use.

PRINCIPLE #4: BE SUBMISSIVE

God's will also covers being submissive. No, this doesn't mean only the wives; I'm talking about Peter's clear teaching, which advises everyone to "submit yourselves for the Lord's sake to every authority instituted among men: whether to the king, as the supreme authority, or to governors, who are sent by him to punish those who do wrong and to commend those who do right. For it is God's will that by doing good you should silence the ignorant talk of foolish men" (1 Pet. 2:13–15).

In so many words, Peter is telling us, "Obey the law." But are we sure we are hearing Peter correctly? Submit ourselves to *every* authority, *every* law of man? What if we don't agree? And what about that scene in Acts where Peter and the other apostles were hauled into court and ordered to quit preaching and teaching about Christ? Didn't Peter say, "We must obey God rather than men" (Acts 5:29)?

There might be those times when we have to choose between obeying God and the government, but Peter isn't talking about that here in his letter. He is talking about being a good citizen, and thus a good witness for Christ. That's why he goes on to say, "Live as free men, but do not use your freedom as a cover-up for evil; live as servants of God. Show proper respect to everyone: Love the brotherhood of believers, fear God, honor the king" (1 Pet. 2:16–17).

I talked with one fellow while visiting a prison. He came up after I preached and told me what a fine message it was, that he had been a Christian for years, and so on. So I asked him why he was doing time and he explained that he had failed to pay 30 traffic fines, plus a few other things, all the while professing Christianity. As kindly as possible, I told him that until he could get his life shaped up, it would probably be better if people didn't know he was a Christian. It's true that God's grace can easily supersede 30 traffic tickets, but this man's inconsistency and apparent insincerity were being a poor testimony, to say the least.

Not only are we to pay our taxes, obey the speed limits and support the other laws of the land, but Peter also talks about being submissive on the job: "Slaves, submit yourselves to your masters with all respect, not only to those who are good and considerate, but also to those who are harsh" (1 Pet. 2:18). Granted, most people don't have to live in slavery today, but then again some of us work for employers whom we fondly refer to as slave drivers. No matter, says Peter, submit anyway. Why? To be a good advertisement for Jesus Christ.

If we are going to be Christians and do God's will, submission is part of the package. We live in an ungodly system and it is God's will that we try to live as exemplary people. And that not only includes obeying laws and obeying employers. It also includes, Peter says, showing respect to everyone. Dr. Harold L. Fickett, Jr.,[6] and I were speakers together at a Bible conference.

I heard him tell a story that nicely illustrates the need to be less belligerent, less uptight and just plain more agreeable people.

It seems this Christian fellow was driving along the street when someone pulled up behind him and started pounding on his horn.

Beep, beep, beep!

Apparently our Christian friend wasn't driving all that fast and he probably thought he had "some impatient jerk" behind him who wanted to get by.

Beep, beeeep, beeeeeep!

So he started fuming and finally couldn't stand it any longer. They came to a red light and he stopped, jumped out, ran back to the "mad honker" on his tail, and said, "If you don't quit blowing that horn, I'll . . ." About then the guy in the other car said, "Oh, I'm sorry. I saw your bumper sticker, 'Honk if you love Jesus,' so of course I honked!"

It's as true with this submissive principle as it was with the others. If we are looking for God's specific guidance and are not being the kind of citizens we ought to be, the kind of employees we ought to be, or the kind of people we ought to be in relating to others, we are missing it. We are to obey God's clearly stated will: be saved, Spirit-filled, sanctified and submissive. The rest takes care of itself.

Principle #5: Suffer for His Sake

The fifth and last thing God's Word says about His will is that we are to suffer. Almost all of us think we might qualify here. We say, "I suffer, with my wife, my husband, my mother-in-law, my kids." The pastor says he suffers with his deacons and the deacons say they suffer with their pastor. Most of us can find something that causes us suffering to some degree.

Sorry, but Peter isn't talking about our everyday discomforts and frustrations. Peter wrote his two letters to Christians who were suffering for their faith. That's why he says, "Dear friends, do not be surprised at the painful trial you are suffering, as though something strange were happening to you. But rejoice that you participate in the sufferings of Christ, so that you may be overjoyed when His glory is revealed. If you are insulted because of the name of Christ, you are blessed, for the Spirit of glory and of God rests on you. If you suffer, it should not be as a murderer or thief or any other kind of criminal, or even as a meddler. However, if you suffer as a Christian, do not be ashamed, but praise God that you bear that name . . . So then, those who suffer according to God's will should commit themselves to their faithful Creator and continue to do good" (1 Pet. 4:12–16,19).

If you're not getting along with your spouse, or your relatives, or your pastor, it's more than likely partly your fault. What Peter is talking about is *suffering for well-doing*—living a godly life in an ungodly society. Do that and you are bound to get some flack. When you go out and really confront the world boldly for Jesus Christ and suffer, that is God's will.

Granted, few of us, in the Western world at least, know much about suffering for Jesus, including myself. I did get one taste of it, however, when I preached on a secular junior college campus on the topic "Christianity and Culture." I talked on culture for a while and then switched to talking about why Jesus is the Messiah. It was a predominantly Jewish student body, so that seemed appropriate to a discussion of culture. It turned into a pretty exciting meeting, with all kinds of antagonistic people there. But I stuck my neck out and trusted God and told it like I believe it is.

In the next few days I got letters with threats to bomb the church. One phone caller told us they would blow up the church during a Sunday service. I got obscene phone calls at home in the middle of the night.

Through the entire experience I got a taste of suffering, but the best part was that some people got saved. I remember in particular a young fellow named Dan, who came to see me not long after hearing my message on "Christianity and Culture." I led him to Christ and he became a key member of our fellowship.

Although we are not seeking to suffer, we must be willing to take a stand, and if we suffer, the Spirit and glory of God rests on us.

To Sum It Up

There is a lot of concern and confusion about God's will, but it is not an unsolvable mystery and it is not the cause of bizarre behavior. God's will is not lost,[7] nor is it the brass ring that some people catch and some people miss, and it really doesn't matter anyway.

There are many good formulas and systems for learning God's will, but the best system is simply what the Bible teaches plainly to be His will:

· He wants us to be saved (see 2 Pet. 3:9).
· He wants us to be Spirit-filled (see Eph. 5:15–18).

- He wants us to be sanctified (see 1 Thess. 4:3–4).
- He wants us to be submissive (see 1 Pet. 2:13–15).
- He wants us to be willing to suffer for His sake (see 1 Pet. 4:12–19).

About now you might be saying, "All these biblical principles are fine, but they're awfully general. What about taking a new job, picking a mate, buying a new car or house, and the millions of other decisions that involve my Christian walk and testimony?"

Well, I've got one other principle for doing God's will and it may sound too good to be true. If you are saved, Spirit-filled, sanctified, submissive, and willing to suffer, do you know the next step? *Do whatever you want!*

Whatever you want? That's right, because if you are going to God's Word to take care of the five areas discussed in this chapter, God is *already* controlling your wants and desires. He is at work "in you to will and to act according to his good purpose" (Phil. 2:13).

Some Personal Questions

1. Of the five biblical principles discussed in this chapter, which ones are of most concern to you regarding God's will, and why?

2. In several places, this chapter stresses that if you are failing to obey the five major principles clearly stated in Scripture as God's will, don't expect much specific guidance

about what to do in a certain situation. Do you agree or disagree? Why?

3. This chapter includes the statement "The Spirit-filled life is living every moment in the conscious presence of Jesus Christ." Why is this difficult for most of us? Does the solution suggested—saturating your mind with God's Word—sound like it would work for you? Why or why not?

4. According to the last paragraph of this chapter, if you are seeking to do God's will in the five major ways discussed, you can do whatever you want in specific areas. What is the strength in that idea? What are possible dangers?

KEY VERSES TO KEEP IN MIND

Understand what the Lord's will is. Do not get drunk on wine, which leads to debauchery. Instead, be filled with the Spirit.

Ephesians 5:17–18

For it is God who works in you to will and to act according to his good purpose.

Philippians 2:13

CHAPTER 8

GOD'S WORD: THE WAY TO GROW

Have you ever seen something or someone that didn't grow? It's a sad sight, for example, to come upon someone 30 years old with the mind of a baby and still in diapers. Because of brain damage or some other mental handicap, some people just don't develop. Their bodies grow to some extent, but they remain virtual infants as far as the rest of their growth and maturity are concerned.

Something almost as disheartening is to see Christians who do not develop. Spiritually they remain stunted, never becoming what God has in mind for them to be. If you challenge these believers, they will deny that their goal is little or no growth. (In fact, they may indignantly argue that they *are* growing—at their own pace!) Everybody wants to grow; it's just that some people want to grow with no effort, and that's where the problem lies.

While I was in college, I wasted my time and didn't grow spiritually very much, if at all. But when I got to seminary I got a taste of God's Word in a new and different way. During those seminary days I learned to study the Bible systematically, and that's when I began to grow. Ever since that time I have found that my spiritual growth is directly proportionate to the

114

amount of time and effort I put into the study of Scripture. Many Christians to whom I've ministered or with whom I have worked would agree.

When believers aren't growing, it can usually be traced to failure to be in God's Word. They go to church and sit. They take along their cups and fill them up and then spill them on the steps as they leave. They complain of not getting much out of church or the Christian life. They are weak and rundown when it comes to facing temptations, trials, problems and challenges. They lack the pep to do much of anything for the Lord.

Their souls are starved for wholesome spiritual food. The Bible refers to itself as milk, bread and meat, but spiritually a lot of Christians are subsisting on French fries, Cokes and M&Ms. They aren't growing because they have very little to grow on. Ironically, the solution to their problems is in the very thing they refuse to feed upon—God's Word.

HOW TO EAT RIGHT AND GROW SPIRITUALLY

There are several excellent biblical passages that talk about spiritual growth, but perhaps the best, and certainly the most basic, is in 1 Peter. Peter wrote two New Testament letters to Christians under intense persecution. Because they had been preaching that the world would be destroyed by fire, the Roman authorities were suspicious of their motives and saw them as a threat to the security of the Empire. But the thrust of Peter's message to them is clear: Don't worry. Put your hope in Christ and learn to live in the light of that, not under your present circumstances.

The Christian believers who read Peter's letters probably weren't too concerned about growing very much "under the present circumstances." They were concentrating on plain old survival. Yet, early in his first letter, Peter tells them that part of the reason they can have hope is because of the living Word of Christ:

> For you have been born again, not of perishable seed, but of imperishable, through the living and enduring word of God. For "all men are like grass, and all their glory is like the flowers of the field; the grass withers and flowers fall, but the word of the Lord stands forever." And this is the word that was preached to you. Therefore, rid yourselves of all malice and all deceit, hypocrisy, envy, and slander of every kind. Like newborn babies, crave pure spiritual milk, so that by it you may grow up in your salvation, now that you have tasted that the Lord is good (1 Pet. 1:23–2:3).

One of the many statements that the Bible makes concerning itself is that it is a "living Word." In Philippians 2:16, Paul calls it the "word of life." Hebrews 4:12 says, "The word of God is living and active." Here in 1 Peter 1:23, it is "the living and enduring word of God." There are no more significant or more important statements that refer to the Bible than these. It is through this living Word that we are born again and made alive spiritually. And it is through the living Word that we grow up into Christ.

THE WORD OF GOD IS ALIVE AND PRODUCES LIFE

The Word of God is the only thing we know of, apart from the Trinity itself, that is alive in an eternal sense. In the world around us, the things we call "living" are really dying. What we call "the land of the living" is probably better named "the land of the dying," because wherever you look, death is doing its work of decay and destruction. In the final analysis, death is the monarch of this world. Against this background of decay and death, the Word of God stands forth as really being alive. The corruption of this world cannot touch God's Word; it cannot remove its validity; it cannot deteriorate its reality; it cannot decay its truth.

God's Word is alive in a truer sense than you and I are alive. As Peter quotes Isaiah 40:6–8, "For, 'all men are like grass, and all their glory is like the flowers of the field; the grass withers and the flowers fall, but the word of the Lord stands forever'" (1 Pet. 1:24–25).

One of the many indications of the life in God's Word is its perennial freshness. In every generation, to every person who picks it up, it is alive, living and fresh. I have reread some parts of the Bible many, many times. I would hope that I had them memorized and would never need to look at them again, but in many cases I am just beginning to understand what they say. I once read the book of Colossians every day for 90 days and, after all of that, the book of Colossians still holds mysteries for me that I haven't tapped. Every time I read the book of Colossians, I gain new excitement and fresh insights.

Something else that says God's Word is alive is that it is never obsolete. In the back of libraries you can find all of the old obsolete textbooks. In recent years, scientific discoveries make dozens and even hundreds of books obsolete each day. But the timeless truths of the Bible never become obsolete. They are as up to date as the next generation of men and women that needs its message so desperately.

And one of the most convincing reasons to call the Word of God alive is its power. The Bible is a discerner of hearts. Scripture has a living insight into me that makes me shake. Through the Bible the Holy Spirit is able to split me wide open and reveal to me my faults, my needs, my weaknesses—and my sins. No wonder Hebrews 4:12 tells us, "The word of God is . . . sharper than any double-edged sword, it penetrates even to dividing soul and spirit . . . it judges the thoughts and attitudes of the heart."

Most important, the Word of God is alive because it produces growth. As 1 Peter 1:23 points out, "You have been born again, not of perishable seed, but of imperishable, through the living and enduring word of God." The great mystery of any living thing is its power to reproduce. And reproduce, says Peter, is exactly what the Word of God does. The only way to be a "son of God" is to be born by the Word of God. When the Word of God is truly heard, and sincerely received into a heart that has been prepared by God, that Word, quickened by the Holy Spirit, becomes a spiritual seed that is imperishable or incorruptible. That seed is the germ of a new creation and it springs into life by making the hearer who believes that Word a son of God.

Jesus illustrates the same concept in His parable of the sower in Luke 8. The farmer goes out to sow and some seed lands on the path, some on rocky soil, some where weeds spring up and some on good ground that produces manyfold. As He explains the parable to His disciples, Jesus says, "The seed is the word of God. Those along the path are the ones who hear, and then the devil comes and takes away the word from their hearts, so that they cannot believe and be saved" (Luke 8:11–12).

The one ingredient a person must have to believe and be saved is God's Word! Naturally, it is the one ingredient that Satan wants to take away. If Satan fails to take it away, life results. Note Jesus' words in Luke 8:15: "But the seed on good soil stands for those with a noble and good heart, who hear the word, retain it, and by persevering produce a crop."

For one more scriptural confirmation of the power of the Word to bring life, see John 6:63: "The Spirit gives life; the flesh counts for nothing. The words I have spoken to you are spirit and they are life." The Word of God, in the hand of the Holy Spirit, is the critical life-giving agent. The Spirit of God, using the Word of God, produces life!

How to Get Off
the Spiritual Junk Food

One reason so many Christians suffer from spiritual malnutrition is that they live on a diet of "junk food" as far as building spiritual character is concerned. Peter is well aware of this and that's why he says, "Therefore, rid yourselves of all malice and all deceit, hypocrisy, envy, and slander of every kind" (1 Pet. 2:1). The *King James* translation of this verse tells us to "lay aside" all of these negative things. The Greek word used here actually means to "strip off your clothes."[1] It's the same thing that is meant in Hebrews 12:1 where we are told to "throw off everything that hinders and the sin that so easily entangles." Peter talks about five specifics that we should strip out of our lives: malice, deceit, hypocrisy, envy, slander.

"Malice" was the general word for "wickedness." In biblical days it meant "heathen evil"—the characteristic evil of the world surrounding the young Christian church. Peter doesn't advise laying aside some of it; he wants it all to go. Today's Christians are no different than those in the first century. Many of us like

to play at Christianity and keep worldly practices and values in our lives. But there is no place in the Christian's life for the garbage of the world.

A young man once approached a great Bible teacher and said to him, "Sir, I'd give the world to know the Bible as you do."

The teacher looked him in the eye and said, "And that's exactly what it will cost you!" If we want to grow, if we want to develop to our full potential, then each of us has to look inside to recognize those worldly remnants and scraps that we are hanging on to, which are hampering growth and maturity.

All deceit (or guile) also has to go, says Peter. At the root of deceit are impure motives and this leads to conscious deception of others. But deceit always costs you in the long run, while honesty always pays.

This is a hard lesson to teach children. I used to tell my own children, "It's really a lot more expensive to lie, because every time I catch you in a lie you are going to be punished much more severely than if you told me the truth." I had to prove this on occasion, and it was always a hard lesson for everyone—for me to teach and for them to learn—but it was worth it.

Hypocrisy is another piece of unneeded junk food. Hypocrisy is a natural outgrowth of deceit and being a phony. Non-Christians always like to point out that the church is full of hypocrites, and unfortunately they are right.

Christians reply to this charge by observing that the church—where people can hear the gospel and be taught the Bible in the right way—is the best place for hypocrites to be. But as Peter plainly shows us, we can't be content with just saying, "It's good to be in church where we're learning to deal with our hypocrisy, deceit and malice." Never be content with keeping this garbage in your life. Strip it off! There is no place in the life of a sincere Christian for hypocrisy. If the Christian glibly excuses his hypocrisy, he is taking advantage of God's grace and is a bigger hypocrite than ever.

Envy is a fourth negative item that has to go out of the Christian's spiritual diet. Reduced to its basic components, envy is simply self-centeredness. Envy is always the last thing to die, because it only dies when the self dies. But as most Christians know, the self is hard to kill.

How many churches have been wrecked, how many missionary organizations have been riddled with dissension, how many families have been destroyed—all by envy? In his letter, James joins Peter in warning the Christian about the demonic influence of envy: "But if you harbor bitter envy and selfish ambition in your hearts, do not boast about it or deny the truth. Such 'wisdom' does not come down from heaven but is earthly, unspiritual, of the devil. For where you have envy and selfish ambition, there you find disorder and every evil practice" (Jas. 3:14–16).

Slander of every kind (evil speaking) is a fifth junk-food dish that has to go. In a word, Peter is telling us, "Quit your gossiping." Gossip just might be the most attractive sin for Christians. We all clatter concernedly over gossip and we nod vigorously when the preacher condemns it from the pulpit, and on the way home or even while walking to the car we engage in it in any number of ways. We are very clever, of course, to mask it behind words like, "I'm so concerned about Mary" or "Can you fill me in a little so I can pray about it?" Far too much gossip goes on under the guise of prayer.

It is worthwhile to note how all of these five items of "spiritual junk food" seem to go together on one big menu. They seem to feed each other as they feed the Christian who keeps them in his diet. The fruit of malice (worldliness) is very often deceit or guile. And deceit and guile lead to hypocrisy, which produces the fruit of envy. And the fruit of envy often leads to evil speaking—slanderous gossip. The trouble is, of course, that like all junk food, this garbage tastes good. We've acquired a real taste for it and it's hard to break the habit. What we need is to start feeding on something else to change our taste buds, and that's what Peter talks about next.

FEED ON GOD'S WORD AND GROW

The obvious replacement for junk food in anyone's diet is something wholesome and nourishing. Peter knows that the cure for spiritual malnutrition is regular feeding on God's Word and that's why he says, "Like newborn babies, crave pure spiritual milk, so that by it you may grow up in your salvation, now that you have tasted that the Lord is good" (1 Pet. 2:2–3). Peter is telling his readers they have tasted God's grace by taking that first step into salvation. The imperishable seed has sprouted and now they need to feed the new life they have within. For the new Christian especially, God's Word is like milk. Milk is crucial to the growth of any baby and God's Word is crucial to the growth of the new Christian.

Paul had the same idea when he wrote to the Christians at Thessalonica and said, "But we were gentle among you, just as a nursing mother cherishes her own children" (1 Thess. 2:7, *NKJV*). Paul has the same idea when writing to Timothy to encourage him to stand fast in the face of apostasy. He tells Timothy that, if he is faithful in instructing the brethren in the truth of God's Word, "You will be a good minister of

Jesus Christ, nourished in the words of faith and of the good doctrine which you have carefully followed" (1 Tim. 4:6, *NKJV*).

As important as milk is, however, the human body needs other foods to gain all its proper nutrition. While some Christians are doing pretty well with laying off spiritual junk food, they are perhaps too content with a weekly bottle fed to them by their preacher. They are failing to get into the Word of God for themselves where they can chew on more solid food.

True spiritual nourishment for the believer is God's Word. However, as Paul told the Corinthians, there is more to God's Word than just milk (see 1 Cor. 3:1–2). The milk helps us get a good start with our growth but we finally need to get to more solid food, the rich spiritual truths that God wants us to have if we are to truly change and become what He wants us to be.

EAT ALL OF GOD'S WORD AND WATCH YOURSELF CHANGE

Not only do most Christians want to grow, but they also want to be different—what the Bible calls renewed or transformed into stronger, more powerful, more effective servants of Christ. That is exactly what Paul is talking about in Romans 12:2 when he says, "Do not conform any longer to the pattern of this world, but be transformed by the renewing of your mind." As every Christian well knows, the old mind, with its habits of self-preoccupation, its craving for sensation and vain imaginations and its appetite for what is cheap and gross, is still there.

The old mind is the culprit that keeps us going back to the junk food. The old mind is the subtle enemy that keeps us feeding only on milk when we should be going on to meat.

The old mind is what keeps us from being transformed and being more committed to Christ and His Word. We keep going around and around and never seem to find the secret. That is because the key to the mystery lies right under our noses.

Paul gives us a beautiful explanation in 2 Corinthians 3:14–18. As he describes the glories of the new covenant that Christians have with God, he goes back to the time of Moses and the Israelites. At one point, after being in God's presence, Moses' face shone with such brilliant glory that he had to put a veil over it in order not to blind his people. But as glorious as Moses' ministry of the law to the Israelites was, Paul says that it does not compare with the surpassing glory of the gospel of Christ and the new covenant that He installed with His death and resurrection (see 2 Cor. 3:7–11).

And Paul goes on to say that since we have such a wonderful hope in Christ, we can be very bold: "We are not like Moses, who would put a veil over his face to keep the Israelites from gazing at it while the radiance was fading away. But their minds were made dull, for to this day the same veil remains when the old covenant is read" (2 Cor. 3:13–14). What Paul is simply saying here is that the Jews of his day who didn't know Christ remained with their minds veiled. They could not see the Lord because the veil of the old covenant—the Law—stood in the way.

Paul goes on to say that it (the veil) "has not been removed, because only in Christ is it taken away. Even to this day when Moses is read, a veil covers their hearts. But whenever anyone turns to the Lord, the veil is taken away. Now the Lord is the Spirit, and where the Spirit of the Lord is, there is freedom" (2 Cor. 3:14–17).

And then Paul comes to the thought that I am most concerned with: "And we, who with unveiled faces all reflect the

Lord's glory, are being transformed into His likeness with ever-increasing glory, which comes from the Lord, who is the Spirit" (2 Cor. 3:18). And so Paul tells us that we can be changed into the image and glory of the Lord. It is very simple, he says. We don't change ourselves. We just stand staring into the face of Jesus Christ and the Spirit of God does the transforming for us!

But you may feel there is just one hitch. You may be saying, "If I'm supposed to look on the glory of the Lord, where do I find it to look upon?" And, of course, the answer to that is in *God's Word*.

If you keep learning and beholding the glory of God in His Word, the Spirit of God will transform you into the image of Jesus Christ. It is just that simple (and just that difficult). So many Christians are seeking some shortcut to growth. In recent days, they have even been trying to make quantum leaps over to "super spirituality." But the shortcut simply doesn't exist.

The greatest thing that ever happened in my life, next to my salvation, was the day I learned to study God's Word. I find that the longer, the more intensely, and the more devotedly I look into the glory of Jesus Christ through the pages of Scripture, the more the Spirit of God changes my life into the image of Christ. There are no shortcuts. If I am to grow, to mature, and to finally be transformed, I must feed on the Word of God!

TO SUM IT UP

Lack of growth is a sad thing to see in anyone or anything. It is especially tragic in Christians, but unfortunately too many believers don't seem to be growing very much in their faith.

The major cause of their lack of growth is failure to be in God's Word.

In 1 Peter 1:23–2:3, the great apostle compares God's Word to two things that are vital for life and growth: an imperishable seed and the milk of the Word. As Christ taught in His parable of the sower, God's Word is like a seed that brings about the new birth. Just as a seed contains the power and energy of life, so too does God's Word.

Before the Christian can get the most from feeding on God's Word, he or she needs to get rid the "junk-food diet" that is so tasty and attractive because of the old nature that all believers still have with them while in this life. Peter describes this junk-food diet as the evils of worldly malice, the guile of deceitfulness, the phoniness of hypocrisy, the self-centeredness of envy, and the slander of gossip. If we want to change our diet, we should start with the sincere milk of the Word of God, and we are guaranteed to grow.

Our goal is to become fully mature and transformed through feeding on the more solid food to be found in Scripture. An accurate description for any Christian can be found in Jeremiah 15:16: "When your words came, I ate them; they were my joy and my heart's delight, for I bear your name, O Lord God Almighty."

SOME PERSONAL QUESTIONS

1. Do you agree or disagree that some Christians might subconsciously set a goal of little or no growth in their spiritual lives? What kind of a goal have you set?

2. In what way is God's Word alive in a truer sense than you and I are alive?

3. In 1 Peter 2:1, the apostle tells us to "strip off" malice, deceit, hypocrisy, envy and slander (gossip). Which of these is the biggest problem for you? Why? What steps might you take to strip it off?

4. Scripture teaches us to go beyond milk to bread and meat in our spiritual lives. At what level are you feeding right now? How might you go beyond this?

KEY VERSES TO KEEP IN MIND

For you have been born again, not of perishable seed, but of imperishable, through the living and enduring word of God.

1 Peter 1:23

Like newborn babies, crave pure spiritual milk, so that by it you may grow up in your salvation.

1 Peter 2:2

When your words came, I ate them; they were my joy and my heart's delight, for I bear your name, O Lord God Almighty.

Jeremiah 15:16

✻✻✻

GOD'S WORD: THE PERFECT PRUNING KNIFE

✻✻✻

How much fruit are you bearing in your Christian life?

Whenever I ask believers a question like that, I often get blank or guilty looks. Some are not sure what I mean. Fruit? They don't own an orchard; they're lucky if they can keep the rust off the rose bushes. Others think I want them to whip out a list of souls won to Christ this month, and because their list is quite short—or nonexistent—they feel guilty.

What, then, is Christian fruit? Does it have something to do with the fruit of the Spirit? Just how does a Christian bear fruit in daily living? And what part does God's Word play in all this?

HE IS THE VINE; WE ARE THE BRANCHES

The classic biblical passage on bearing fruit is John 15:1–8. Jesus and His disciples are in the Upper Room on the night before His death. As they are about to leave, the Lord stops and says:

I am the true vine and my Father is the gardener. He cuts off every branch in me that bears no fruit, while every branch that does bear fruit he trims clean so that it will be even more fruitful. You are already clean be-cause of the word I have spoken to you. Remain in me, and I will remain in you. No branch can bear fruit by itself; it must remain in the vine. Neither can you bear fruit unless you remain in me.

I am the vine; you are the branches. If a man remains in me and I in him, he will bear much fruit; apart from me you can do nothing. If anyone does not remain in me, he is like a branch that is thrown away and withers; such branches are picked up, thrown into the fire and burned. If you remain in me and my words remain in you, ask whatever you wish, and it will be given you. This is to my Father's glory, that you bear much fruit, showing yourselves to be my disciples (John 15:1-8).

Here is one of the most meaningful and, at the same time, most difficult analogies in the entire Bible. Here also is one of the richest passages in the New Testament on living the Christian life.

First, we need to get a basic explanation of what Jesus means. He is the vine and His Father is the gardener—or vinedresser. The disciples are the branches. He is referring to the 11 disciples who are still with Him as He prepares to go to the Garden of Gethsemane. They are the branches who are abiding or remaining with Him to the end. The branches who don't bear fruit and are cut off are represented by Judas, who has already left to complete his act of treachery by telling the Jewish leaders where they can find and seize Jesus later in the evening. Jesus uses the vine illustration for at least three good reasons:

First, His disciples will recognize the analogy immediately because Israel was often referred to as a vine in the Old Testament Scriptures. For example, Isaiah wrote, "The vineyard of the Lord Almighty is the house of Israel" (Isa. 5:7). Jeremiah, speaking for God, said, "I had planted you like a choice vine of sound and reliable stock" (Jer. 2:21).

Second, grapevines grew everywhere in Palestine. Some commentators, in fact, believe Jesus stopped at the doorway on His way out of the Upper Room to refer to a vine growing by the doorway.[1] When He spoke of pruning procedures, He was describing exactly what vinedressers did to produce good crops of grapes. Young vines were pruned severely for their first three years, and then were allowed to bear a crop. Mature vines were pruned every December and January. Non-fruit-bearing branches were cut back mercilessly to preserve the strength of the plant. And, as Jesus pointed out in His analogy, the wood of the pruned branches was good for nothing except making bonfires.[2]

Third, the vine and its branches perfectly illustrate the kind of relationship that must exist between Jesus and anyone who wants to be His disciple. Although Jesus was addressing His inner circle of 11 disciples, this analogy is for all Christians. Jesus is saying we have a choice: to be "for real" branches who truly remain (abide) with Jesus and bear fruit, or to be phony un-productive branches who seem to be in the vine but are not. Like Judas, they fade away and produce no fruit at all. And, like Judas, their ultimate fate is destruction.

It's important to note that Jesus says, "I am the *true* vine." In the Old Testament, Israel had been referred to often as a vine planted, tended and pruned by God, but Israel had become unproductive. In fact, the symbol of the vine used in Old Testament passages always refers to the idea of degeneration. Hosea cries that Israel is "an empty vine" (Hos. 10:1, *KJV*). Now, with the Old Testament order ending and the new covenant just installed at the Last Supper, Jesus states clearly that He is the true vine. It is to Him that God's children must now be related. For anyone to know life and bear fruit, he or she must be connected to Jesus Christ.

THE WORK OF THE GARDENER

The task of the gardener (or vinedresser) is crucial to understanding the vine/branches analogy. The gardener is the Father who has two ministries concerning the branches on the vine (those who claim allegiance to Jesus Christ).[3]

Any vinedresser has two duties: to cut off branches that bear no fruit, and to prune the fruit-bearing branches in order to help them bear even more and richer fruit.

The word "prune" also means to purge or to cleanse. The vinedresser would do his cleaning of the fruit-bearing branches in various ways. Sometimes he would use his thumb and forefinger to pinch away the growing tip of a vigorous but unwanted shoot. Or he would "top" the branch, lopping off a foot or two to keep it from growing too large or too long and possibly snapping off in the wind. Maybe he would thin the vine, which meant removing unwanted flower clusters.

In all these processes, the vinedresser was after one thing: the good of the plant and aiding that plant to bear more and better fruit.

When applying this picture of the vinedresser's work with an actual grapevine to the Father's work with us, we see that there are two kinds of branches: those who claim to follow Christ but are not true believers; and those who truly believe, if only a little bit, and who bear at least some fruit in their lives. The fate of the non-fruit-bearing branches gives us an awesome warning. Those who are "Judas branches," those who do not really believe in and remain with Christ, are to be cast into eternal fire. It is not a question of their losing their salvation. They were never really saved in the first place. Sooner or later they show their real colors and their end is destruction.

True believers, however, always bear fruit. I believe that every Christian bears some kind of fruit. It may not be much; with some Christians you may have to look a long time to find a few lingering grapes, but they are there. If there is no fruit at all, that person is not a true Christian. The entire essence of the Christian life is that it is to be productive in some way (see Eph. 2:10). A person may look as if he is connected to Jesus Christ. He may even have a lot of luxuriant greenery in his life; but if he doesn't bear any fruit, he is not really connected to Christ at all.

The Father's work with the fruit-bearing branches is another matter. Here He carefully prunes the Christian, trimming away sins, hindrances, habits, and so on, in order to help that Christian gain maximum fruit-bearing capacity.

One of the most effective ways the Father prunes the Christian is with trouble, even pain and suffering. This is not to say that every Christian who is ill or suffering is necessarily being pruned, but in many cases the Father allows trial and trouble to come our way in order to clean out our lives in certain areas.

Unfortunately, pruning has to be done with a knife, and a knife is painful. There are times when we wonder if God knows what He is doing because it hurts so much it seems more than we can bear. And why is it God seems to do an awful lot of pruning on our branch while other Christians seem to get along with very little pruning at all? But all we can do is trust. The Father knows what He is doing. The valuable lessons He teaches us through suffering, trials and troubles awaken us to the necessary changes we need to make, what we need to add to our lives and what we need to remove.

The Father causes this pruning in many ways. It can be anything from sickness to hardships such as loss of a job. It can be the loss of a loved one or of a good friend. Pruning can come through frustration, disappointment, pressure and stress. God ordains the kind of trouble that cleans off the suckers, those un-wanted shoots and the other things that get into our lives to drain away our energy and rob us of fruit-bearing capacity. God doesn't do this pruning with glee or vengeance. He is not the Great Slasher in the Sky, flailing away with His giant blade, snarling, "Bear more fruit, or else!" No, He is right at our side, working carefully to prune each of us at the right spots so that we can bear more fruit.

The pruning knife may hurt now and then, but it's worth it. Have you ever thought about what the Father's pruning knife actually is? Is it suffering? Troubles? Frustrations? I don't think so. John 15:3 tells me the pruning knife is the Word of God. Jesus says, "You are already clean because of the word I have spoken to you."

I believe that here in verse 3 Jesus is referring to two kinds of cleansing for His disciples. First, their initial salvation comes through hearing the Word. Second, their continual purging and pruning is done by the Word. That is why His next words are "Remain in me, and I will remain in you. No branch can bear fruit by itself; it must remain in the vine. Neither can you bear fruit unless you remain in me" (John 15:4).

And just how do we remain in Christ and have Him remain in us? *By being in the Word.* There are no substitutes, no gimmicks or shortcuts. God's pruning knife is His Word, and as pointed out above, He seems to use it often during trouble, distress or setbacks of some kind.

Charles Spurgeon, master preacher of the nineteenth century, said, "It is the Word that prunes the Christian. It is the truth that purges him."

Have you ever noticed how much more sensitive you are to the Word of God when trouble comes? Have you ever noticed that, when you have a particular need or problem, certain verses will practically leap off the page? That's the Spirit of God applying them to your heart.

WHAT CHRISTIAN FRUIT IS NOT

With all this pruning and purging going on, it makes sense to be sure we know what kind of fruit we are supposed to bear. One thing is basic: For the believer in Christ, bearing fruit is a requirement, not an option. The Old Testament talks about it at least 70 times. Paul talks about it in all of his letters in one way or another.

But what kind of fruit do Paul and other writers of Scripture describe? First, let's take a quick look at what Christian fruit *is not*, because some people get certain kinds of plastic fruit confused with the real thing.[4]

Fruit is not success. Nowhere in the Bible is fruit synonymous with success. We all have the tendency to think if something is big, or if a lot of people are coming, that means it is bearing fruit. Not necessarily. A big "successful" operation could be a performance of the flesh—human effort—but not real spiritual fruit at all.

On the other side of the coin, we look at the missionary who has worked for 30 years in some backwoods, up-the-river or out-in-the-desert station and see that he has three converts to his credit. It is entirely possible that his work has borne real fruit, despite the outward lack of "success."

Fruit is not sensationalism. We also tend to be impressed with the flashy, the spectacular, the overly zealous. The emotional pitch and the ringing rhetoric all promise, "Here is real fruit!" But talk is cheap; real spiritual fruit is expensive.

Fruit is not simulation. A subtle trap ensnares many Christians when they try to imitate the actions or style of another believer who is apparently bearing fruit in his or her ministry. But all Christians are to bear their own fruit. They are unique and so is the fruit they bear. When Christians try to simulate or imitate somebody else's fruit, they violate the basic principle of abiding in Christ. Instead of living in Christ and allowing Christ to live in and bear fruit through them, they are figuratively tying on plastic fruit. It may look good but the taste is flat.

WHAT IS REAL CHRISTIAN FRUIT?

Scripture describes genuine spiritual fruit in several ways, and I place them in a certain order of priority for an important reason.

First, fruit is Christlike character. Paul put it in one sentence in Galatians 5:22: "The fruit of the Spirit is love, joy, peace, patience, kindness, goodness, faithfulness, gentleness and self-control." This list describes the character traits of Jesus Christ. We are to reproduce the life of Christ in us as we abide in the vine. Jesus said, "I am the vine; you are the branches. If a man remains in me and I in him, he will bear much fruit; apart from me you can do nothing." To underline the absolute necessity to be in Christ—to be a "for real" branch—Jesus repeats the grim warning He gave in verse 2: "If anyone does not remain in me, he is like a branch that is thrown away and withers; such branches are picked up, thrown into the fire and burned" (John 15:6).

But to bear the fruit of the Spirit, or any other kind of Christian fruit, we must understand one thing. The way to the fruit is through Christ. One of the most frustrating tasks in the world is to try to bear the fruit of the Spirit on our own. We look at our lives and see that we are a bit short on love. So, we grunt and groan and try to produce more love. Or we detect that we are a bit short on peace, so we work so hard at producing more peace that we are more uptight than ever!

Jesus doesn't tell us to "Get out there and bear more fruit!" He simply says, "Abide . . . remain with me and the fruit will appear of its own accord."

A second description of fruit is praising the Lord in worship. Hebrews 13:15 tells us, "Through Jesus, therefore, let us continually offer to God a sacrifice of praise—the fruit of lips that confess his name." As we thank God in a spirit of worship, fruit is present. As we pray and express adoration to the Lord, that is fruit. But note that all of this is done "through Jesus," not ourselves.

A third kind of fruit is good works. We often shy away from the idea of "works" because we know that we are saved by grace, not works, lest any of us might boast that we did it, not God (see Eph. 2:8–9). But we forget that Paul goes right on to say that "we are God's workmanship, created in Christ Jesus to do good works, which God prepared in advance for us to do" (Eph. 2:10). We are not saved by our works, but we are saved to do good works in Christ's name. That is why, in his letter to the Colossian Christians, Paul tells them (and us), "For this reason, since the day we heard about you, we have not stopped praying for you and asking God to fill you with the knowledge of his will through all spiritual wisdom and understanding. And we pray this in order that you may live a life worthy of the Lord and may please him in every way: bearing fruit in every good work, growing in the knowledge of God" (Col. 1:9–10).

Note again that Paul is praying that God will fill the believer with the knowledge of His will, with spiritual wisdom and understanding. As we are filled by God, we can dispense good works that bear real fruit. And we are filled by staying close to Christ—remaining in Him.

Finally, the Christian bears fruit by winning others to Christ. A key passage that identifies those won to Christ as fruit is found in John 4. Jesus' disciples plead with Him to stop to eat, but Jesus replies that His food is doing the will of His Father and accomplishing His work. Then Jesus says, "Do you not say, 'There are yet four months, and then comes the harvest'? Behold, I say to you, lift up your eyes, and look on the fields, that they are white for harvest. Already he who reaps is receiving wages, and is gathering fruit for life eternal" (John 4:35–36, *NASB*).

Unfortunately, some believers think the best way to reap the harvest is to wade in and try to mow down as many converts as possible. But the way to bear fruit as a soul winner is not by running around buttonholing people, dropping tracts on the table for the waitress instead of a tip. Instead, remain (abide) in Christ. Let Him build His character in you and the opportunities will come. Concentrate on Him and He will place you in witnessing situations designed especially for you.

The other approach—do-it-yourself soul winning—is a dead end. I got a taste of this while taking a summer college course in evangelism. Our assignment was to witness to seven people a week. The instructor didn't set a quota on how many we had to get converted in order to earn an *A*, but we were required to witness to seven people a week in order to get a grade at all.

It was legalism pure and simple, but it taught us one thing: the folly of witnessing "because you have to" and the obvious common sense of abiding in Christ and witnessing out of an overflow of knowing and loving Him. That is why fruits of Christlike character, praising God and good works should come first. If we aren't enjoying these fruits and seeing them fulfilled in our lives, the answer is painful, but obvious: We aren't abiding enough. We are not in the Word enough—written or living.

DO GOD'S WORDS CONTROL YOUR LIFE?

If we are to be real, not phony, branches, we must let the words of the Lord control us. And what are the words of the Lord? Do we all need to memorize the red-letter portions of red-letter Bibles? That's not a bad idea, but the words of Christ are not limited to quotes attributed to Him in red-letter editions of the Bible. As we saw in the early chapters of this book, all of Scripture has infallible, inerrant authority for our lives. What Jesus said personally is no more important than what He said through Paul, Peter, James, Jude and other writers of inspired

Scripture. But to simply talk about "being controlled by the Word of God" remains only so much talk unless we can say we are actually familiar with it. There is no magic in memorizing Scripture. (In fact, it can lead you into the driest kind of legalism.) But there is tremendous blessing and power in knowing where various passages can be found and what kind of help and resources they can provide.

For example, the following is a brief quiz containing 12 basic Scripture passages that should be familiar to a Christian. See if you can match the right passage with the right description:

The Ten Commandments	Luke 10
The Love Chapter	Matthew 22:34–40
The Beatitudes	Matthew 5–7
The Parable of the Good Samaritan	Exodus 20
The Two Great Commandments	1 Corinthians 13
The Sermon on the Mount	Matthew 5:1–12
The Call of Abraham	Luke 6:31
The Fall of Man	Genesis 12
The Golden Rule	Luke 15
The Parable of the Prodigal Son	Genesis 3

Correct answers are listed at the end of this chapter. See how you did at matching. Then try covering up one column or the other and getting the right answers from memory. Remember, memorizing verses and references can be a legalistic "head trip," if you make it that. On the other hand, just what does it mean to know Christ's Word well enough to be under His control? Unless we are in the Word, reading it, memorizing it, learning it, knowing it, all of our talk about abiding and fruit-bearing is just hot air.

According to John 15:8, there is a marvelous blessing in being pruned to bear more fruit: "This is to my Father's glory, that you bear much fruit, showing yourselves to be my disciples." The believer who bears fruit through his relationship to Christ and not his own efforts and cleverness—that believer brings glory to God.

Here is the bottom line. To paraphrase the well-known answer to the first question in the Westminster Confession: He is the Vine; we are the branches.[5] By staying with Him and in Him, we shall glorify God, enjoy Him forever and show the world we are His disciples!

TO SUM IT UP

Jesus gives us the secret of bearing fruit when He tells us that our relationship to Him must be like branches in a vine. If we are real branches, truly attached to Him in genuine faith, we will bear fruit, if only a little bit. In order to help us bear more fruit, the Father uses the Word to purge and prune the unneeded habits, attitudes and practices from our lives. He often works through trouble—anything from illness and loss to frustration and stress. His pruning knife is painful, but it is worth it.

Plastic fruit is a danger Christians must avoid. Real fruit is not necessarily success or sensationalism. Real fruit is not gained by simulating the ministry of another Christian who is bearing fruit. Every Christian is to bear his or her own fruit.

The Bible describes real fruit in several ways: (1) as Christ-like character (the fruit of the Spirit); (2) as praise through worship; (3) as being fruitful in every good work. A fourth important kind of fruit is converts won to Christ, but witnessing for Him should come out of abiding (remaining) in Him, not legalistic effort.

The benefits of being pruned are many. Bearing fruit brings happiness, joy, satisfaction and excitement. We also experience answers to prayer as our lives are regulated by God's Word. The total result is that we bring glory to God as we know and enjoy Him forever.

SOME PERSONAL QUESTIONS

1. Do you agree that one of the most effective ways God uses to prune our lives is through trouble and adversity? What other ways might He use?

2. According to this chapter, what is the crucial difference between plastic fruit and the real thing? Have you ever tried simulating the fruit of another Christian who had an effective ministry?

3. Can you recall at least three of the four kinds of fruit this chapter describes? In your opinion, which ones are most important?

ANSWERS TO THE MATCHING QUIZ

The Ten Commandments—Exodus 20
The Love Chapter—1 Corinthians 13
The Beatitudes—Matthew 5:1–12
The Parable of the Good Samaritan—Luke 10
The Two Great Commandments—Matthew 22:34–40
The Sermon on the Mount—Matthew 5:6–7
The Call of Abraham—Genesis 12
The Fall of Man—Genesis 3
The Golden Rule—Luke 6:31
The Parable of the Prodigal Son—Luke 15

KEY VERSES TO KEEP IN MIND

*I am the vine; you are the branches. If a man remains in me and
I in him, he will bear much fruit; apart from me you can do nothing.*

John 15:5

*But the fruit of the Spirit is love, joy, peace, patience, kindness,
goodness, faithfulness, gentleness and self-control.*

Galatians 5:22

CHAPTER 10

God's Word:
The Ultimate Weapon

At one time, one of the more famous scenes in the history of television was a sequence that used to run almost weekly on the *Wide World of Sports*. As thrilling feats of athletic prowess flashed on the TV screen during this classic show, the announcer droned on about how he and his camera crews were "spanning the globe to bring you the constant variety of sports—the thrill of victory . . ."

At this moment the camera caught a fearless ski jumper hurtling gloriously down the incline—

". . . and the agony of defeat."

Suddenly the jumper goes out of control, hurtles off the side of the jump before he even has a chance to become airborne, smashes through several signs and other apparatuses and cartwheels on down the slope to what seems certain death. Fortunately, it turned out that he was not hurt as badly as it appeared, and he was able to return to action later.

We all identify with that jumper because we, too, have known the agony of defeat. I don't know about you, but I prefer to win. I don't like to lose. From the time I was big enough to lift a bat or a football or a schoolbook, my dad taught me that "If you're going to do it, do it to the best of your ability or don't do it at all."

I grew up trying to follow my dad's philosophy, always striving for excellence whenever I could. I don't like to be on the bottom. I prefer the top. And this philosophy carries over into my Christian life. I am not interested in beating fellow Christians (or non-Christians for that matter) at any cost, but I am interested in defeating Satan. I don't like to see Satan win anything. And I don't like to see the world master me. I don't like to see the flesh override the Spirit. When it comes to the world, the flesh and devil, I like to win as many rounds as possible.

I used to have a football coach who would give us the classic Knute Rockne lecture at halftime, Rockne being the man whom some regard as the greatest football coach of all time. One of his favorite sayings was, "You can't be beat if you won't be beat." I think Christians could use a motto like that as they go into daily spiritual combat. According to the Scriptures, we have the necessary equipment to gain victory. In fact, we have the ultimate weapon—the sword of the Spirit. All we need is the will to win.

THE MOST IMPORTANT PIECE OF ARMOR

Most Christians are familiar with the famous "spiritual armor" passage in Ephesians 6. In his famous analogy, written while he was chained to a Roman soldier, Paul is describing equipment that is vital, not optional. The daily battle with Satan, not to mention the world and the flesh, is real, as anyone who has been a believer for more than 30 minutes can tell you. Each piece of the Christian's armor is worth at least one chapter in any book, but here we are concentrating on that final item—the sword of the Spirit, God's authoritative Word.

To fully understand Paul's concept of the sword, we need to take a brief look at Greek terms. Paul does not use the Greek word for "sword," *romphaia,* which stood for a huge weapon with a blade of 40 inches or more. The *romphaia* was the great broad two-edged sword soldiers would wield with two hands. With a *romphaia,* you were not interested in precision work. You flailed away with abandon and hoped you hit something.

Instead, Paul uses a very common Greek word, *machaira,* which describes a weapon that could be anything from a six-inch dagger on up to an 18-inch sword easily wielded in combat to make defensive parries and attacking thrusts. The *machaira* was the kind of sword carried by most Roman soldiers in hand-to-hand combat.[1]

This word *machaira* is used in Matthew 26:47 to describe the weapons in the hands of the soldiers who came to arrest Jesus in the Garden of Gethsemane. It is the same word used when Peter's sword sliced off the ear of the high priest's servant. *Machairas* were for precise work. If Peter had used a *romphaia,* the poor fellow would have probably ended up in two equal pieces!

Note that Paul calls it the sword *of the Spirit.* I believe that he is basically referring to where the sword comes from—in this case from the Holy Spirit. There is a crucial difference between possessing the sword of the Spirit and simply possessing the Bible. An unbeliever can possess a Bible, but it does him little good. As we saw in chapter 2, the natural man does not understand the things of God. But when we believe in Christ, we receive the resident truth-teacher—the Holy Spirit. It is the Spirit of God in the life of the believer who makes the Word of God available and effective in the believer's life. Every Christian possesses the sword of the Spirit. How well he or she knows how to use it is the question.

But Ephesians 6:17 has still more to tell us. Paul says we need the sword of the Spirit, *the Word of God*. We have already seen that Paul was thinking of the *machaira* kind of sword, small and easily used in a precise way. He does not mention the *romphaia*, the huge broad sword that required two hands and mighty unguided swings. The Greek that Paul uses here for "word" is not *logos*, the standard definition for God's general revelation of Himself. Instead he uses the word *rema*, which refers to *specific statements*.

The principle that Paul is clearly presenting in Ephesians 6:17 is that when using the sword of the Spirit, we need to be specific. When temptation comes we cannot simply wave the Bible in the air and say, "God's Word will protect me!" We need to know which part of God's Word fits the situation. We need to know how to use the sword of the Spirit on defense and on offense.

HOW'S YOUR DEFENSE?

If you have ever watched a sword fight, you know that a sword is used as much to parry (turn aside) a blow as it is to deliver one. Without an adequate defense the swordsman would quickly be cut down. The same principle applies to using God's Word in spiritual warfare. The Christian's first responsibility is to learn to use the sword of the Spirit with defensive skill. Satan attacks with constant temptations, but you can literally parry his blows with the proper use of God's Word.

Jesus gives His classic lesson in defensive strategy in the account of how He was tempted by Satan in three ways (see Matt. 4 or Luke 4). It's worth noting that the temptations came to Jesus right after a moment of spiritual triumph. At His baptism by John, the Spirit of God descends on Him like a dove and His Father's voice is heard saying, "This is my Son, whom I love; with him I am well pleased" (Matt. 3:17). And in the next sentence we see Jesus in the wilderness, being tempted by the devil. The same thing can happen to any believer. As we experience a spiritual victory, we can be misled into thinking Satan can't touch us ever again. But what seems like victory can quickly turn to defeat. Every moment brings new challenges. The battle never ceases.

The wilderness that Jesus entered for His battle with Satan was an area between the central plateau of Jerusalem and the Dead Sea. Called "the devastation" in the Old Testament, it is a territory of unbelievable barrenness, rocks, heat and dust. Jesus spent 40 days out there—alone—and then the tempter came.

Satan's first temptation was very basic. After fasting for 40 days and nights, Jesus was obviously hungry. "If you are the Son of God," said Satan, "turn these stones into bread" (see Matt. 4:2–3). Jesus looked at the thousands of rounded stones lying at His feet, each one looking like the rounded loaves baked in Palestinian ovens.[2] Was this simply an invitation to indulge His ravenous appetite? Surely the heavenly Father might forgive that, under the circumstances. But there is much more at stake here. The first word Satan uses is "If." *If* Jesus is the Son of God, surely He can do as He pleases. Surely God's Son should not have to want for food. Satan is saying, "You're God's Son, so satisfy yourself. Why wander around out here any longer, unhonored, unattended, starving for what purpose? Is this befitting the Son of God? Use your power and authority and set things right!"

But Jesus recognizes the temptation for what it is: an invitation to distrust God and use His own power and authority to satisfy His wants. His answer is brief, precise *and straight from an Old Testament passage in Deuteronomy*: "Man does not live on bread alone, but on every word that comes from the mouth of God" (Matt. 4:4; see Deut. 8:3).

Satan's first blow is parried, but he's just getting warmed up. Since Jesus likes to quote Scripture, so will Satan (something for every Christian to keep in mind). His next suggestion is that Jesus cast Himself off the roof of the Temple at Jerusalem, a fall of over 300 feet. After all, the angels will catch Him, just as it says in Psalm 91. Again, Jesus' answer is right on target, and from the Scriptures: "It is also written: 'Do not put the Lord your God to the test'" (Matt. 4:7). In this case Satan was not only tempting Jesus to be sensational to attract followers, he was also suggesting that He see how far He could go with the Father. God expects us to take risks to be true to Him, but not to take risks to enhance our own prestige.

Two of Satan's thrusts have been stopped cold, but he is still swinging. With his next offer he pulls out all the stops.

Jesus can have all the kingdoms of the world, if He will just bow down and worship the devil. All He really would have to do is "compromise a little" and play the game—relate to the worldly system a little more; be relevant and contemporary instead of straight and old-fashioned. But Jesus wields the *machaira* again and quotes for the third time from that old book called Deuteronomy: "Away from me, Satan! For it is written: 'Worship the Lord your God, and serve him only'" (Matt. 4:10; see Deut. 6:13).

Jesus is so fed up with Satan's ploys that He tells him to vamoose, and he does just that. Three times the devil gives Jesus his best swing, and three times he fails. The reason? Jesus uses the sword of the Spirit in just the precise way needed. Since all three of Jesus' answers came from Deuteronomy, we might wonder if that's the only book He knew. Hardly. He used Deuteronomy three times in a row, *because it fit each situation*. He could have just as easily quoted Psalms, Proverbs, Genesis—whatever fit.

The principle is very clear. When defending yourself from Satan's attacks, use the *machaira* of the Spirit, the *rema* of God, to specifically parry each blow. The Christian has to be able to defend himself at whatever point the temptation appears. He has to have the principles, the passages and the truths of God's Word in his heart and mind. He can't always take time to stop and ask the pastor at the church door, or to dial a prayer. If the Christian can't parry the blow himself, Satan will score, and the Christian will lose that round.

And never doubt it for a minute—Satan has a way of knowing where you're weak. You may be able to fake it in a Bible study discussion or even with a Jehovah's Witness at your door, but you don't fool Satan. He will attack at your weakest point. You can never know enough of how to use the sword of the Spirit. It is all too easy to fall to temptation simply because you don't know how God's Word deals with the questions and problems that come at you every day.

AND DON'T FORGET TO GO ON THE OFFENSE

As much as I use God's Word to defend myself against Satan's attacks, I love to use it as an offensive weapon. That's when things get exciting. Staying on the defensive all the time gets old, but when I start using my sword of the Spirit on offense I see myself whacking away at some of the jungle of Satan's kingdom.

And how do you use God's Word on offense? Every time you take the gospel to an unsaved person, the sword of the Spirit cuts a swath through Satan's kingdom of darkness. Every time you teach or share the Word in your family, in a class, among your friends, or on the job, you are slashing away at the undergrowth Satan uses to trap his prey.

Satan knows God's Word is effective and that's why he tries to stop it whenever he can. In chapter 9 we saw the Word compared to seed, which Satan does his best to take away or choke out with weeds or rocks (see Luke 8). We have also noted that the Word is quick and powerful, so sharp it cuts us wide open to reveal our real motives (see Heb. 4:12).

In Jeremiah 23:29, God asks, "Is not my word like fire . . . and like a hammer that breaks a rock in pieces?" And who can forget Paul's bold, totally-on-the-offensive statement in Romans 1:16: "I am not ashamed of the gospel, because it is the power of God for the salvation of everyone who believes."

But using the sword of the Spirit on offense is the same as using it for defense. You have to make specific moves and precise thrusts. Have you gotten into a conversation and couldn't come up with answers because you didn't know what the Bible teaches in that area? That doesn't mean we should take refuge behind the "silent curtain." Better to admit you don't know. Then go find out, so you can wield your sword more precisely and effectively the next time. The more we know the Word, the better we can march through Satan's kingdom, cutting right through his core of lies.

ARE YOU A BUTTERFLY, BOTANIST OR BEE?

One of the common excuses Christians often give for not knowing the Word better than they do is that they "don't understand it." I don't buy that. God not only gave us His Word, but He also planted His resident truth-teacher—the Holy Spirit—in our hearts. He will teach us if we want to learn. G. Campbell Morgan, a pulpit giant of the nineteenth century, was approached by a man after preaching a stirring sermon. The man blurted, "Dr. Morgan, your preaching is such an inspiration!" Morgan is reported to have replied, "Ninety-five percent of inspiration is perspiration." That's right. It takes work to master the Bible, work done with skill and accuracy. Our sword of the Spirit is a *machaira*, not a *romphaia*.

An old but graphic illustration tells of a man who looked out of his window at a beautiful garden full of plants and flowers. First, he saw a lovely butterfly, which would flutter from flower to flower, pausing for only a second or two before moving on. It touched many of the lovely blossoms but derived no benefit from them.

Next he spotted a botanist, with a big notebook under his arm and a large magnifying glass in his hand. The botanist would hunch over one flower for a long time, peering at it through his magnifying glass and scribbling furiously in his notebook. He stayed for hours, studying flowers and writing notes. Finally he closed his notebook, put his magnifying glass in his pocket and walked away.

The third visitor to the flower garden was a tiny bee. The bee would light on a flower and sink down deep, extracting all the nectar it could carry. On each visit to a flower it went in empty and came out full.

And so it is with Christians in their approach to God's Word. There are the butterflies who move from stirring sermon to stirring sermon, from Bible class to Bible class, fluttering here, fluttering there, bringing nothing and gaining nothing but a nice feeling. And there are the spiritual botanists who take copious notes. They are trying to get everything straight—from each vowel point to each point in the outline. They go over the words but don't draw much out of the flowers. It's all pure academics.

And then there are the people who are like spiritual bees. They sink down deep into every flower, every book or page of Scripture they come upon, and draw out the wisdom and truth and life that can be a blessing to them and those around them.[3]

Which one are you? It's easy to spot the trouble with the butterfly, but the botanist's problem is more subtle. After all, isn't careful study of the Word what it's all about? Careful study of God's Word *is* what it's all about, *if* it goes beyond your head and gets into your heart. The difference is obedience to the Holy Spirit, your resident truth-teacher, who can give you full benefit from God's Word if you give Him free rein. You will come in and go out full—again and again and again. You will know how to use your sword of the Spirit, on defense, on offense, in any way needed. And in the daily spiritual battle, you will have your fair share of the thrill of victory!

TO SUM IT UP

Every Christian possesses the equipment necessary to gain victory in the daily struggle against the world, the flesh and the devil. A crucial weapon is the sword of the Spirit, the Word of God, which is likened to a small, easily wielded weapon used for close precision work. This sword is given by the Holy Spirit, who is the resident truth-teacher in every Christian's heart. It is the Word of God, which must be used specifically and precisely to be effective in the believer's life.

The two uses of the sword of the Spirit are defensive and offensive. On defense we must learn to use the Word to parry the blows and thrusts of Satan, who is always trying to tempt us at our weakest point. On offense we must be just as specific and precise as we wield the sword by teaching and sharing God's Word wherever we can to cut a swathe through the devil's dark kingdom.

There are three approaches to God's Word that can be likened to three visitors to a beautiful flower garden. We can be butterflies who flutter about, getting little of real value; or botanists who carefully study the details and the fine points of the flower but who fail to find any real nourishment. Or we can be bees, who sink deep into God's Word, going in empty and coming out full of His truth, wisdom and power.

How we choose to use our sword of the Spirit determines the margin we will know between the thrill of victory and the agony of defeat.

SOME PERSONAL QUESTIONS

1. Would you say you use the sword of the Spirit better on offense or defense? Why?

2. Can you think of three areas where you might learn to use the sword of the Spirit more skillfully? Here are some ideas:

   · On defense—in ethical decisions, in moral situations (i.e., control of sexuality), in temptations to gossip and slander, when confronting your pride, your hunger for power, pleasure or materialism.

   · On offense—in witnessing, in talking about the Lord with your family, in standing for Christian principles without coming off as a prude or obnoxious, in teaching others about Christ by example or through direct instruction.

3. Which visitor to the flower garden most accurately identifies you most of the time? Butterfly? Botanist? Bee? Why is it easier sometimes to be a botanist than a bee? Why is it sometimes hard to tell the two approaches apart?

KEY VERSES TO KEEP IN MIND

Take . . . the sword of the Spirit, which is the word of God.

Ephesians 6:17

Man does not live on bread alone, but on every word that comes from the mouth of God.

Matthew 4:4

PART III

HOW TO GET THE MOST FROM GOD'S WORD

It is helpful to know why we can trust the Bible and why it has authority beyond any other book (see chapters 1 to 5). And it is motivating to see what the Bible can do for us, as it gives us power for daily living (see chapters 6 to 10). But the authority and power of Scripture will do us little good if we do not use it properly and regularly.

The value of God's Word is unquestionable, but how to read and study it effectively and consistently remains a mystery to many. But the mystery can be solved if we want to solve it. Getting the most from God's Word involves basic questions:

- *What does God's Word say?* What is the best way to read it? How much per day, per week? What are the best techniques for remembering what you read?

- *What does God's Word mean?* What is the best approach to interpreting the Bible? Can the typical layperson find the real meaning of Scripture? What is the best method for studying God's Word with profit?

In these last two chapters, we will be taking a look at practical ways to get as much from God's Word as we can.

CHAPTER 11

WHAT DOES GOD'S WORD SAY?

If the previous chapters of this book have accomplished anything, they have demonstrated again and again that in the Bible all Christians have an incredible treasure. Effective study of the Word of God is basic to the Christian life. At the core of everything for the Christian is knowledge of God's Word.

PREREQUISITES FOR WORTHWHILE BIBLE STUDY

If we want to know God through His Word, it is vital to have the right attitude of heart and mind. Effective Bible study takes at least five things: new birth, real desire, constant diligence, practical holiness, and prayer.

New birth, being born again, seems obvious, but it is vital. As we saw so clearly in chapter 2, in order to get anything out of God's Word, you have to belong to God. The natural man doesn't understand God's truths because he lacks the resident truth-teacher, the Holy Spirit (see 1 Cor. 2:14).

Real desire to know the Word is crucial. In recent decades there has been a great deal of stress on emotionalism, on getting some kind of charge out of Christianity. But you don't primarily come to the Bible for a feeling. The Scriptures are not a sanctified pep pill. The Scriptures are there to give you knowledge, and gaining that knowledge takes effort. The more you want to make that effort, the more you are going to gain from Scripture.

Halfhearted Bible study is a bore. If you come to the Scriptures legalistically or ritualistically or because you're intimidated by your peers or your pastor, you won't get much out of it. What you need is a hunger in your heart, a passion for knowing God through His Word. Ask yourself how badly you want to know God. Where is this "want" on your priority list?

Constant diligence comes right on the heels of real desire. Your wants have to result in action or nothing will happen. There is no avoiding it; studying the Bible is hard work. The Holy Spirit is not going to zap us as we stroll through the park or slouch in front of the TV set. The Spirit works through the Word and we have to work to get His message for us.

In addition to a myriad of duties as pastor of a large church, I spend some 25 to 30 hours per week in sermon preparation. To be honest, there are days when I don't feel as diligent as I would like. The passion to know God burns at a lower ebb. It would be a lot more fun to take the family to the beach, take in a ball game, or just relax at home with the paper and some favorite magazines. At times like that I have to remember the Berean Christians in Acts 17. Luke calls them noble because they searched the Scriptures daily (see Acts 17:11). Second Timothy 2:15 tells me, "Do your best to present yourself to God as one approved, a workman who does not need to be ashamed and who correctly handles the word of truth." Bible study takes discipline. If there is no perspiration, there will be no inspiration.

Practical holiness is a fourth prerequisite that we don't dare ignore.
I call it "practical" because I simply mean having a cleaned-up life. I can talk about holiness in very spiritual and mysterious terms, but the bottom line is "How pure is my life?" In chapter 8 we saw the key to growth as *first* laying aside (stripping off) malice, deceit, hypocrisy, envy and gossip and then going to the sincere milk of the Word to grow as Christians (see 1 Pet. 2:1–2).

If you insist on practicing certain favorite sins, the sincere milk of the Word won't set all that well. You will wind up with indigestion or, more often than not, you will decide you are just not hungry.

Prayer is another crucial element of Bible study. The early apostles reduced their priorities to two: "We . . . will give our attention to prayer and the ministry of the word" (Acts 6:4). Scripture study and prayer just supernaturally go together. Prayer is seeking the divine Source of understanding—God Himself.

The apostle Paul underlined the centrality of prayer in gaining biblical understanding when he wrote, "I have not stopped . . . remembering you in my prayers. I keep asking that the God of our Lord Jesus Christ . . . may give you the Spirit of wisdom and revelation, so that you may know him better. I pray also that the eyes of your heart may be enlightened" (Eph. 1:16–18).

Paul sensed deeply the need for divine enlightenment through revelation from God, and he sought it through prayer. No Christian believer should ever look down at the Word without first looking up at the very source of that Word and asking for guidance. To engage in Bible study without prayer is presumption, if not sacrilege.

Having looked over some of the prerequisites for worthwhile Bible study, let's move on to just how it's done. The first step is simple—perhaps too simple.

READ GOD'S WORD SYSTEMATICALLY

The first step in Bible study is to *read the Bible*. I can't emphasize too strongly that effective Bible study has to begin with a systematic reading of the Scriptures. Other methods will be of limited benefit unless you get the entire flow and context of what God's Word is saying.

With all of the Bible study tools, methods and resources on the market today, Christians are always tempted to make the same mistakes as did the Jews of the southern kingdom of Judah when Isaiah prophesied their destruction at the hands of foreign invaders. They scoffed at Isaiah's warnings, as if they were mere Sunday School moralizing. They thought they were far above and beyond the principle that "precept must be upon precept, precept upon precept; line upon line, line upon line; here a little, and there a little" (Isa. 28:10, *KJV*). Their end is well known. Judah fell to the Babylonians in 586 B.C., and the scoffers who thought they were beyond the fundamentals and the basics were marched into captivity.[1]

The point is well made: No believer is ever beyond the basics. Sophisticated and ingenious Bible study methods and books are fine, but they should never come ahead of fundamental steps, and there is no more fundamental step than systematically reading God's Word, line upon line, precept upon precept, absorbing its total truth and cohesiveness.

A PLAN FOR THE OLD TESTAMENT

Of course you need a plan for your reading. For the Old Testament I suggest reading through all of it once a year in a narrative manner (from Genesis to Malachi, no skipping around). True, there are some difficult portions. The going is a bit heavy through Leviticus and parts of Deuteronomy, but by and large the Hebrew language of the Old Testament translates into very simple, concrete reading.

I have studied Hebrew and Greek and the difference between them is significant. Greek is an intensely complex language and is often difficult to interpret because of its philosophical nature. It is an abstract way of saying things. Hebrew, on the other hand, is very concrete, earthy and simple.

And the best way to read the Old Testament is straight through, like a story. Don't look for a presentation of systematic theology. Don't start by looking for "types" and allegories and dispensations. You can do that later, after you get into Bible interpretation (see chapter 12). But first simply read the Old Testament to see what it says, to hear the story it has to tell. You will see the unfolding of God's progressive revelation and you will also discover foundations for New Testament truths that come later.

As you read, keep a pencil and notebook in hand. Put down notes regarding areas you want to come back to and study in depth later, preferably with the inductive method (see chapter 12). When you come to a passage you don't understand completely, don't let it bog you down. Put a question mark in the margin and move on. As you continue to read the Old Testament year by year, line upon line and precept upon precept, you will begin to erase the question marks.

What is the best way to organize your reading of the Old Testament? How many chapters per day, per week?

One simple plan is this. There are 929 chapters in the entire Old Testament. Divide 929 by 365 days and you come up with just over two-and-a-half chapters a day. To allow for occasional days when you may miss due to illness or other problems, set a goal of at least three chapters a day, which should take an average of 15 to 20 minutes. Keep in mind that some chapters are quite long; others are very short. The average chapter usually takes about a page in a typical Bible, so the goal of three chapters a day is definitely not overwhelming.[2]

A Plan for the New Testament

With the New Testament I use a little different approach. I still keep the principle of repetition from Isaiah 28:9 (line upon line, precept upon precept), but with an important variation. Instead of reading through the entire New Testament from Matthew to Revelation, I read each book over and over for 30 days. This works beautifully with the shorter books, for example 1 John. In fact, I started using this system with 1 John. I read it straight through in one sitting (it took about 30 minutes). Perhaps you have never read an entire book all the way through, even a short one. But reading a book straight through in one sitting gives you the context and flow. It helps get you off the proof-text/ memory-verse syndrome. You already know how I feel about Scripture memorization (see chapter 9). It's important, but unless it's done with an organized approach, such as the one used by the Navigators,[3] it's all too easy to get the idea that the Bible is a collection of nice little sayings.

The Bible has a flow and a context, especially the letters from Paul, James, and others. When somebody writes you a letter, you don't stop to read a nice line, then jump two pages to find another good thought. You read it through to get the flow.

So, sit down and read 1 John through. Are you through? Hardly. The next day read 1 John through in one sitting again. On the third day, do it again, and so on for 30 days. Do you know what happens at the end of 30 days? You know what is in 1 John. Nobody can trip you up. Where does it talk about forgiveness of sins? Chapter 1, verses 7 to 9. Where does John talk about how and why God is love? Chapter 4, verses 7 to 21. For warnings about loving the world too much see chapter 2, verses 15 to 17. For the promise of eternal life see chapter 5, verses 11 and 12.

Those are just a few obvious samples. You'll be able to see 1 John in your mind's eye—the location of every verse, where every line fits. And, best of all, you will have the flow of the book and understand its basic message. Then go on to another short book and do the same thing for 30 days. Always read the book through in one sitting, every day, for 30 days. At the end of 30 days you'll have another New Testament book in your heart and mind as never before.

"Okay, okay," you're thinking, "this is fine for shorter books like 1 John, Colossians or Philippians, but what about longer books like the Gospel of Matthew, the Gospel of John or the Acts of the Apostles? And what about Revelation? If I read that straight through every day for 30 days, I'll be seeing visions, too."

But there's an easy answer to the problem. You break the longer books up and still use the same 30-day system. For example, the Gospel of John has 21 chapters. Divide it into 3 sections of 7 chapters each. Read the first 7 chapters daily for 30 days. Then take the next 7 and read them daily for 30 days, and likewise with the last 7. In 90 days you will cover the Gospel of John with your own custom-made, fine-tooth comb. And I guarantee you will know what's in there. Jesus and Nicodemus? John 3. The first miracle at the wedding in Cana? John 2. The calling of the disciples? John 1. The Vine chapter? John 15. The Good Shepherd? John 10. The Bread of Life discourse? John 6.

If you want to know what the Bible says, this method will do the job like no other. Vary the length of the books you tackle. First a short one, then a long one, then back to a couple of short ones. In two-and-a-half years you will cover the entire New Testament 30 times, and somewhere along the way it will all start to come together as never before. A truth in Colossians will match up with one in Ephesians. Paul's arguments of Romans will clearly relate with his polemics in Galatians. The parable of the Good Samaritan will dovetail with the practical instructions in Romans 12, Ephesians 5 and Galatians 6.

Of course you might be saying, "Oh, this is too hard. I can't possibly keep up a schedule like that. It's easy for John MacArthur; he has to do this 25 to 30 hours a week to prepare his sermons."

There are several answers to this problem. First, this 30 -minutes-a-day-for-30-days approach is worth the effort. It will free you from the bewilderment of so many Christians who pick up the Bible and say, "Oh, help! Look at all this. I can't possibly absorb all this or make much sense out of it. I'll let the pastor sort it out and feed it to me in bite-size pieces." And that's where they stay, being spoon-fed instead of really knowing the Word for themselves.

As for keeping it up, yes, it will take discipline. And you may get bored. For some people the boredom comes at the seventh day or the twelfth day or the nineteenth. Part of the reason for this is that you will still be reading the Bible as you always have—somewhat superficially. The way to fight boredom is to look deeper into what you're reading. Begin to really search out what the writer is saying. Read slower, not faster. Soon you will find yourself saying, "Oh, I see! Ah, this makes sense! Now I get it."

Yes, you may have days when you don't pull it off. You may miss your reading due to illness, emergencies or traveling. But the system is what counts. As best you can, *stick to the system*. Read each book or portion all the way through as often as you can on a daily basis, but be flexible. On some days perhaps you should spend more time at prayer. Let the Holy Spirit guide you in developing a personal Bible reading system that works best *for you*.

One other point. If you want to get serious about Bible reading and study, you will have to reset your priorities. All of us have to fight laziness and inertia. To do anything worthwhile you have to pay a price. As a student in seminary, I heard leading scholars and students of the Bible explain how to study the Bible. They all virtually said the same thing: *read the Scriptures repetitiously*.

Your first goal is to find out what the Bible says. There is a second important step—finding out what it means. We'll take that up in the last chapter.

TO SUM IT UP

To know God—really know Him—through His Word is a vital goal for every Christian. To know God so that He actually speaks to us through His biblical message takes regular, effective Bible study. To make study of the Bible worthwhile,

How to Get the Most from God's Word

we need: the new birth, real desire to learn, constant diligence, practical holiness, and prayer.

The first step in worthwhile Bible study is to read the Bible. That may seem too obvious and simple, but unless we are reading the Bible regularly and systematically, we will learn little. Bible study tools and resources have their place, but they should never replace going over and over the Scriptures, line upon line, precept upon precept.

A good plan for reading the Old Testament is in narrative style, straight through, with no skipping around. This way you cover its entire story of progressive revelation. With the New Testament a good plan is to cover its new covenant truths by reading the same book every day for 30 days to get its flow and become completely familiar with its truths. With larger New Testament books divide them into sections and cover a section each day for 30 days. For example, you can cover the 21 chapters in the Gospel of John by doing 7 chapters for 30 days, then 7 more for another 30 days, and the last 7 over another 30 days.

Is the read-a-book-daily-for-30-days system too difficult? While you might miss a day now and then, it is well worth the effort. In two-and-a-half years you will know God's Word as never before.

SOME PERSONAL QUESTIONS

1. How do you see the Bible? (a) as a treasure of inestimable value; (b) as something full of wisdom and practical help; (c) as a somewhat difficult book that you know you are

168

supposed to study. How do you explain your attitude toward the Scriptures? Where do you think you got it?

2. In your opinion, what is the difference between knowledge *about* God and knowledge *of* Him?

3. On a scale of 1 to 10, with 10 being best, how do you rate your desire to know the Word?

4. How does the read-a-book-daily-for-30-days plan strike you? Are you willing to try it? What would be the major obstacles? The major benefits?

KEY VERSES TO KEEP IN MIND

I want to know Christ and the power of his resurrection.

Philippians 3:10

Precept upon precept . . . line upon line . . .
here a little, and there a little.

Isaiah 28:10, *KJV*

CHAPTER 12

WHAT DOES GOD'S WORD MEAN (AND WHAT DO I DO ABOUT IT)?

A young couple from another church came to one of our assistant pastors for counseling about marital problems they started having soon after their wedding. After just a few minutes of interviewing the two, he could see they were miles apart in tastes, ideas and opinions.

"What made the two of you get married?" he asked.

"A sermon our pastor preached on Joshua conquering Jericho."

"What did that have to do with getting married?"

"Well," explained the husband, "Joshua and his army claimed Jericho, marched around it seven times and the walls fell down. Our pastor told us that if we trusted God, claimed a certain young girl and marched around her seven times, the walls of her heart would collapse and she would be willing to marry. So, I did it, and we got married."

Our assistant pastor stared in disbelief. Was the husband putting him on? No indeed. In fact, several couples in that particular church had gotten married on the same basis after hearing the same sermon!

The above story illustrates at least two things: (1) You can get completely confused on what the Bible means and what to do about it; (2) the interpretation and application of Scripture can be crucial for life decisions.

THE IMPORTANCE OF CUTTING
IT STRAIGHT

The interpretation of Scripture has been something of a battleground for centuries for an obvious reason! It is all very subjective, or so it seems. Doesn't everyone have his own view and isn't one view as valid as another? Not necessarily. I believe there are sound principles for scriptural interpretation. There are some difficult areas, true. There are some things we'll never all agree on because our information or capacity is incomplete. As Deuteronomy 29:29 so wisely says, "The secret things belong to the Lord our God."

On the other hand, there is an awful lot in God's Word that we can interpret in a sound and orderly manner. As Mark Twain, the crusty agnostic, admitted, "It's not the things I don't understand in the Bible that bother me. It's the things I *do* understand."

The apostle Paul would have agreed with Mark Twain at that point. When he wrote to Timothy, Paul said, "Do your best to present yourself to God as one approved, a workman who does not need to be ashamed and who correctly handles the word of truth" (2 Tim. 2:15). The *King James Version* has it, "rightly dividing the word of truth." The Greek literally says here, "cutting it straight."

171

Paul had been a tentmaker and he may well have used this phrase as he compared the making of tents with the study of Scripture. In Paul's time tents were made in a patchwork design with animal skins. To get all the parts to fit properly, they had to be cut correctly. The same thing is true of Scripture. The Bible is a whole. God has given us the whole tent, so to speak. But if we don't cut straight on the individual pieces (the verses, chapters and books), the whole won't fit together. We won't handle His Word correctly.

The result of "cutting it crooked" can be anything from minor errors to total chaos and confusion. An example of chaos is what cults do as they cut Scripture according to their own crooked patterns. But plenty of crooked cutting goes on in the ranks of biblical Christians, too. Incredible things have been proved or disproved with careless or crooked use of the Bible.

Theologians call the science of Bible interpretation *hermeneutics* (from the Greek word *hermeneuo*). To escape faulty hermeneutics, we should avoid some basic errors.

Making a point at the price of proper interpretation is a common temptation for pastors who want to force the Scriptures to agree with their sermons; but lay people can fall into the same trap. A classic example is the rabbi who took the story of the Tower of Babel and claimed that it teaches us to be more concerned for one another. Why did he come up with that? Because his research in the *Talmud* revealed that as the tower grew taller, workmen carrying loads of bricks to the bricklayers would fall and be killed. Those in charge of the project were distraught when a workman fell on the way up and lost the load of bricks, too. But if a workman fell on the way down with an empty load, it was no big deal. All they lost was a workman.

The crass inhumanity of the tower builders carries a lesson, true, but it is not the lesson in the biblical account of the Tower of Babel, which teaches that God confused the languages of men because they rebelled against Him. God destroyed the Tower of Babel because it was a symbol of idolatry, not because the builders cared more about bricks than people.

In Bible study, get the right message from the right passage. Don't "proof text" your bias or opinions by making the Bible say what you already know you want it to say.

Spiritualizing or allegorizing Scripture is another gimmick ministers will use on lay people—from the pulpit or in their writings. We have already seen one funny, but tragic, example of allegory overkill with the how-to-get-a-mate-with-the-walls-of-Jericho message.

I heard another example of allegory out of control at a conference, where one of the other speakers talked about the eleventh chapter of John and the resurrection of Lazarus. His interpretation: "Lazarus is the symbol of the church, and what we have here is a vivid picture of the rapture of the believers. The resurrection of Lazarus is the church going through the rapture."

Afterward, this speaker came up and said, "John, did you ever see that in the text before?" I tried to be honest but diplomatic: "You know, I doubt that anyone has ever seen that in the text before. You are the first!"

There are passages in Scripture that are symbolic. There are passages that give us types and pictures. But beware of views that read symbols and pictures into the text that simply are not there.

I call this "Little Bo Peep" preaching. You don't need the Bible. You can use Mother Goose, Aesop's Fables or the Yellow

Pages to prove your point. The "reasoning" goes like this: "Little Bo Peep has lost her sheep. What a tragedy to be lost. All over the world people are lost. Who can find them . . ." And so on and on into an allegorical swamp that makes the Slough of Despond look like a well-paved parking lot.

Although there is only one passage in all of Scripture that is plainly identified as an allegory (Paul's use of Hagar and Sarah in Galatians 4:22–31), there are numerous other allegorical or figurative references. Most of these, however, are easy to recognize. See, for example, the Good Shepherd allegory in John 10; and how can we fail to mention the allegory that was our basis of study in chapter 9—the Vine and the branches? Remember, too, that every time you take communion you are acting out the most meaningful allegory in all Scripture (see Luke 22).

The Old Testament offers allegories also. Proverbs 5:15–19 symbolizes marital fidelity by advising that a man drink from his own cistern. (Note also that this allegory is explained in Proverbs 5:20–23.) Another interesting allegory is in Ecclesiastes 12:3–7, where old age is pictured as a household that is functioning with less and less efficiency.

The key to interpreting allegories is to establish if the writer of Scripture *meant it as an allegory*—symbolic or figurative language—to teach a truth. The allegories used by the writers of God's Word are genuine and obvious. Approach all other allegorical interpretation with caution.[1]

PUTTING IT ALL TOGETHER INDUCTIVELY

While it's helpful to know about some of the errors to avoid in Bible study, the key questions for many Christians are still:

"How do I put it all together? How can I work out a Bible study method that will let me work at my own speed and at my own level of ability?"

If you have visited your Christian bookstore lately, you know there are dozens of Bible study helps on the market. You can soon become swamped in reading the titles and, after choosing a book, you can spend hours familiarizing yourself with its contents, and still not really be into actual study of the Bible!

My solution is something you may have heard of—inductive Bible study. "Inductive" means reasoning from the specific to the general, from the parts to the whole. It is the opposite of deductive reasoning, in which you move from the general to the specific.

There are several excellent inductive Bible study books and methods on the market and you may want to examine some of these for yourself. But right here let me give you a simple four-step approach that can get you going immediately in learning to "cut it straight."

Observation is the first step. This involves the major topic discussed in chapter 11—reading the text over and over. As you observe what is being said, here are specific questions to keep in mind as you make notes:

Who is the writer? To whom is he writing? To and from where is he writing? What is the situation or occasion? When did it occur? What historical/cultural factors might have a bearing on understanding the passage?

Keep in mind that there are several "gaps" you will have to hurdle: language, culture and geography. Very often, if you have a good study Bible, such as *The Ryrie Study Bible*,[2] many of the above questions are answered, at least in part, in an introduction printed at the beginning of each book.

Interpretation is the second step. When doing interpretation it is important to *do your own work*. There are certain study tools you can use (see below), but don't resort to commentaries at this point. Dig in and determine what the passage means *to you*, as you do the following:

1. Underline key words and phrases and define them in terms of the context—what the passage is saying. Underline only the most basic and important words at first, then use your Bible dictionary, concordance, word study book, and so on, to study meanings.

2. Paraphrase (put into your own words) each verse or section of the passage. If this grows laborious, try putting the basic thought conveyed in a passage or paragraph into one sentence. This may seem like a lot of work (and for some people it is) but it forces you to think and come up with the meaning in your own words, something that is difficult but very beneficial.

3. List the divine truths and principles in the verse, paragraph or passage. Ask these questions:

   · Is there a command God has given?
   · Is there an example to follow?
   · Is there some sin I should avoid?
   · Is there a warning against false teaching of any kind?
   · Is there a basic doctrinal truth about God, Christ, the Holy Spirit, man, Satan?

· Is there a promise from God to Christian believers, Israel, the church, unbelievers? (Note the conditions of the promise, as for example in Matthew 6:33.)

4. Cross reference as many truths or principles as possible. Do you find these same truths taught in other parts of Scripture? Use your concordance or other tools to find out. List at least one or two, but don't get bogged down with trying to list six, or eight, or twenty.

Evaluation is the third step. Here is where you stop to check what commentators and other scholars have said about the passage. You have already covered this to some extent in doing your observation and interpretation, but go back again to see what divine truths or principles are emphasized by the commentaries in your library. You may modify your own understandings or conclusions, but don't always think you have to agree with every commentator. Make them prove themselves. As somebody once said, "The Bible is a good commentary on the commentaries."

Application is the last step. How can the passage become relevant for *your* life? What does the Lord want you to stop doing? What does He want you to start? What should you be doing more often?

Keep in mind that application of Bible truth does not have to be a profound, life-or-death kind of thing. You can apply God's Word right at home—every morning as you're getting off to work, or every evening during that crucial dinner hour when everybody's tired and hungry. You can apply it at church, in your neighborhood, on the job—anywhere you have relationships with others. It might be interesting to keep tabs on how many applications of Scripture you actually make. Record them in your study notebook. How many do you have after a month? Three months? A year?

All of the other steps and principles in Bible study will be of little use unless we finally employ practical application. That's precisely what Paul was talking about when he told Timothy that all Scripture "is useful for teaching, rebuking, correcting and training in righteousness" (2 Tim. 3:16).

Biblical teaching, or doctrine, is basic. Here we have found out what Scripture says and means. But the final and crucial questions are: So what? What are you going to do about it? How do you use it in your own life?

That's where the rebuking, correcting and training come in. As Scripture rebukes us, it reveals our sin and shows us how and why we should change. Our next step is correcting our course, changing our path, developing new habits. It all adds up to being trained in the Word—disciples in whom the Word of Christ dwells richly as we give thanks to Him (see Col. 3:15–17).

To Sum It Up

Interpretation of Scripture can be a confusing battleground if sound objective principles are not employed. According to 2 Timothy 2:15, the Christian is to learn to rightly divide the word of truth—"to cut it straight" (*KJV*). Examples of cutting Scripture in a "crooked way"—misinterpreting it completely or partially—have been plentiful throughout history.

One basic error that befalls some Bible students is to try to make a point at the price of proper interpretation. In other words, don't proof-text a biased opinion in order to make the Bible say what you want it to say.

Another basic error is spiritualizing or allegorizing Scripture. This Little-Bo-Peep approach allows the imagination to run wild in order to get a "meaning" from a biblical passage. When allegorical language is used in Scripture, it is usually fairly obvious. Trouble starts when Bible teachers, preachers, and others, start allegorizing biblical passages that don't have any allegories in them.

A basic Bible study method is the inductive approach. Key steps in the inductive approach include observation, interpretation, evaluation and, most important, application. Scripture teaches, rebukes, corrects and trains us (see 2 Tim. 3:16) as we let the word of Christ dwell in us richly (see Col. 3:15–17).

SOME PERSONAL QUESTIONS

1. Do you agree or disagree? "All the other steps and principles in Bible study will be of little use unless we finally employ practical application." Write a paragraph explaining your answer.

2. Have you ever used the inductive method of Bible study? Do you believe it would work with your schedule and lifestyle? What changes might have to be made in your priorities in order to do any serious inductive study?

KEY VERSES TO KEEP IN MIND

*Do your best to present yourself to God as one approved,
a workman who does not need to be ashamed and
who correctly handles the word of truth.*

2 Timothy 2:15

*Let the word of Christ dwell in you richly as you teach and
admonish one another with all wisdom.*

Colossians 3:16

Bible Reading
and Study Plans

Following are several suggestions for setting up a daily time for Bible reading and study. These ideas are based on principles discussed in chapters 11 and 12. You may wish to alter them to suit your own tastes and study habits.

Thirty Minutes Per Day

Chapter 11 describes a 30-day New Testament reading plan, which emphasizes reading the same New Testament book or portion every day for 30 days. Chapter 12 describes a four-step plan for inductive Bible study. To get the best results, you need to combine reading and inductive study on a consistent, organized basis. If you are working with only 30 minutes a day, you will not have time to read a New Testament book or portion, do inductive study and have a time of prayer. The answer to this problem is to modify the system by reading the book or portion on one day and doing inductive study on the next day. Here is an example of how this can work, using the letter to the Galatians:

Day 1:   Read entire letter; use remaining or additional time for prayer.

Day 2:   Do inductive study of chapter 1 for 15 to 20 minutes; use remaining or additional time for prayer.

Day 3:   Read entire letter; use remaining or additional time for prayer.

Day 4:   Do inductive study of chapter 2 for 15 to 20 minutes; use remaining or additional time for prayer.

Day 5:   Read entire letter; use remaining or additional time for prayer.

Day 6:   Do inductive study of chapter 3 for 15 to 20 minutes; use remaining or additional time for prayer.

Day 7:   Read entire letter; use remaining or additional time for prayer.

Day 8:   Do inductive study of chapter 4 for 15 or 20 minutes; use remaining or additional time for prayer.

Day 9:   Read entire letter; use remaining or additional time for prayer.

Day 10:   Do inductive study of chapter 5 for 15 or 20 minutes; use remaining or additional time for prayer.

Day 11:   Read entire letter; use remaining or additional time for prayer.

Day 12:   Do inductive study of chapter 6 for 15 or 20 minutes; use remaining or additional time for prayer.

Days 13–30: Repeat the above cycle as often as possible. Vary your inductive study to give yourself extra time in portions of Scripture that are more difficult or rich in meaning. Always, however, spend every other day in reading the entire letter in order to benefit from the principle of learning by repetition.

To do one month of Old Testament study, use the same "alternate days" plan, which would work like this:

Day 1: Read Old Testament book in narrative fashion for 15 or 20 minutes; use remaining or additional time for prayer.

Day 2: For 15 or 20 minutes do inductive study of what you read on previous day. Spend remaining or additional time in prayer.

Repeat this every-other-day system until 30 days are up. You should be able to cover two or three chapters of the Old Testament every two days. Then switch back to study of a New Testament book for the next 30 days.

Sixty Minutes Per Day

If you have 60 minutes per day, you can try to work in the Old and New Testaments during each session, but you will find yourself less rushed if you stay in one Testament for 30 days at a time.

For study of the Old Testament, read for 20 minutes; do inductive study of what you have read for 20 minutes; pray for 20 minutes.

For study of the New Testament, read the entire book or major portion of the book you have chosen. Use the remaining time for inductive study and prayer. To do your inductive study, break down the book or portion as shown in the 30-minute plan. When doing inductive study, never try to cover more than one chapter at a time. As you gain skill in inductive study, you will find that you will want to do shorter sections and even single verses to gain full benefit from the rich truths you will find.

NINETY MINUTES PER DAY

With 90 minutes or more, you have ample time to do Old and New Testament reading and study daily, if you wish to do so. One way to use a 90-minute block of time would be: Read the Old Testament for 15 minutes, then do 15 minutes of inductive study of what you have read. Read the New Testament book or major portion for 20 to 30 minutes (depending on how long it may take); spend 30 to 40 minutes in inductive study and prayer. You may want to vary the use of your time according to your personal needs and interests.

THE CHICAGO STATEMENT ON BIBLICAL INERRANCY

Preface

The authority of Scripture is a key issue for the Christian Church in this and every age. Those who profess faith in Jesus Christ as Lord and Savior are called to show the reality of their discipleship by humbly and faithfully obeying God's written Word. To stray from Scripture in faith or conduct is disloyalty to our Master. Recognition of the total truth and trustworthiness of Holy Scripture is essential to a full grasp and adequate confession of its authority.

The following Statement affirms this inerrancy of Scripture afresh, making clear our understanding of it and warning against its denial. We are persuaded that to deny it is to set aside the witness of Jesus Christ and of the Holy Spirit and to refuse that submission to the claims of God's own Word that marks true Christian faith. We see it as our timely duty to make this affirmation in the face of current lapses from the truth of inerrancy among our fellow Christians and misunderstanding of this doctrine in the world at large.

This Statement consists of three parts: a Summary Statement, Articles of Affirmation and Denial, and an accompanying Exposition. It has been prepared in the course of a three-day consultation in Chicago. Those who have signed the Summary Statement and the Articles wish to affirm their own conviction as to the inerrancy of Scripture and to encourage and challenge one another and all Christians to growing appreciation and understanding of this doctrine. We acknowledge the limitations of a document prepared in a brief, intensive conference and do not propose that this Statement be given creedal weight. Yet we rejoice in the deepening of our own convictions through our discussions together, and we pray that the Statement we have signed may be used to the glory of our God toward a new reformation of the Church in its faith, life and mission.

We offer this Statement in a spirit, not of contention, but of humility and love, which we propose by God's grace to maintain in any future dialogue arising out of what we have said. We gladly acknowledge that many who deny the inerrancy of Scripture do not display the consequences of this denial in the rest of their belief and behavior, and we are conscious that we who confess this doctrine often deny it in life by failing to bring our thoughts and deeds, our traditions and habits, into true subjection to the divine Word.

We invite response to this Statement from any who see reason to amend its affirmations about Scripture by the light of Scripture itself, under whose infallible authority we stand as we speak. We claim no personal infallibility for the witness we bear, and for any help that enables us to strengthen this testimony to God's Word we shall be grateful.

I. SUMMARY STATEMENT

1. God, who is Himself Truth and speaks truth only, has inspired Holy Scripture in order thereby to reveal Himself to lost mankind through Jesus Christ as Creator and Lord, Redeemer and Judge. Holy Scripture is God's witness to Himself.

2. Holy Scripture, being God's own Word, written by men prepared and superintended by His Spirit, is of infallible divine authority in all matters upon which it touches: It is to be believed, as God's instruction, in all that it affirms; obeyed, as God's command, in all that it requires; embraced, as God's pledge, in all that it promises.

3. The Holy Spirit, Scripture's divine Author, both authenticates it to us by His inward witness and opens our minds to understand its meaning.

4. Being wholly and verbally God-given, Scripture is without error or fault in all its teaching, no less in what it states about God's acts in creation, about the events of world history, and about its own literary origins under God, than in its witness to God's saving grace in individual lives.

5. The authority of Scripture is inescapably impaired if this total divine inerrancy is in any way limited or disregarded, or made relative to a view of truth contrary to the Bible's own; and such lapses bring serious loss to both the individual and the Church.

II. Articles of Affirmation and Denial

Article I.

We affirm that the Holy Scriptures are to be received as the authoritative Word of God.

We deny that the Scriptures receive their authority from the Church, tradition, or any other human source.

Article II.

We affirm that the Scriptures are the supreme written norm by which God binds the conscience, and that the authority of the Church is subordinate to that of Scripture.

We deny that church creeds, councils, or declarations have authority greater than or equal to the authority of the Bible.

Article III.

We affirm that the written Word in its entirety is revelation given by God.

We deny that the Bible is merely a witness to revelation, or only becomes revelation in encounter, or depends on the responses of men for its validity.

Article IV.

We affirm that God who made mankind in His image has used language as a means of revelation.

We deny that human language is so limited by our creatureliness that it is rendered inadequate as a vehicle for divine revelation. We further deny that the corruption of human culture and language through sin has thwarted God's work of inspiration.

Article V.

We affirm that God's revelation in the Holy Scriptures was progressive.

We deny that later revelation, which may fulfill earlier revelation, ever corrects or contradicts it. We further deny that any normative revelation has been given since the completion of the New Testament writings.

Article VI.

We affirm that the whole of Scripture and all its parts, down to the very words of the original, were given by divine inspiration.

We deny that the inspiration of Scripture can rightly be affirmed of the whole without the parts, or of some parts but not the whole.

Article VII.

We affirm that inspiration was the work in which God by His Spirit, through human writers, gave us His Word. The origin of Scripture is divine. The mode of divine inspiration remains largely a mystery to us.

We deny that inspiration can be reduced to human insight, or to heightened states of consciousness of any kind.

Article VIII.

We affirm that God in His work of inspiration utilized the distinctive personalities and literary styles of the writers whom He had chosen and prepared.

We deny that God, in causing these writers to use the very words that He chose, overrode their personalities.

Article IX.

We affirm that inspiration, though not conferring omniscience, guaranteed true and trustworthy utterance on all matters of which the Biblical authors were moved to speak and write.

We deny that the finitude or falseness of these writers, by necessity or otherwise, introduced distortion or falsehood into God's Word.

Article X.

We affirm that inspiration, strictly speaking, applies only to the autographic text of Scripture, which in the providence of God can be ascertained from available manuscripts with great accuracy. We further affirm that copies and translations of Scripture are the Word of God to the extent that they faithfully represent the original.

We deny that any essential element of the Christian faith is affected by the absence of the autographs. We further deny that this absence renders the assertion of Biblical inerrancy invalid or irrelevant.

Article XI.

We affirm that Scripture, having been given by divine inspiration, is infallible, so that, far from misleading us, it is true and reliable in all the matters it addresses.

We deny that it is possible for the Bible to be at the same time infallible and errant in its assertions. Infallibility and inerrancy may be distinguished but not separated.

Article XII.

We affirm that Scripture in its entirety is inerrant, being free from all falsehood, fraud, or deceit.

We deny that Biblical infallibility and inerrancy are limited to spiritual, religious, or redemptive themes, exclusive of assertions in the fields of history and science. We further deny that scientific hypotheses about earth history may properly be used to overturn the teaching of Scripture on creation and the flood.

Article XIII.

We affirm the propriety of using inerrancy as a theological term with reference to the complete truthfulness of Scripture.

We deny that it is proper to evaluate Scripture according to standards of truth and error that are alien to its usage or purpose. We further deny that inerrancy is negated by Biblical phenomena such as a lack of modern technical precision, irregularities of grammar or spelling, observational descriptions of nature, the reporting of falsehoods, the use of hyperbole and round numbers, the topical arrangement of material, variant selections of material in parallel accounts, or the use of free citations.

Article XIV.

We affirm the unity and internal consistency of Scripture.

We deny that alleged errors and discrepancies that have not yet been resolved violate the truth claims of the Bible.

Article XV.

We affirm that the doctrine of inerrancy is grounded in the teaching of the Bible about inspiration.

We deny that Jesus' teaching about Scripture may be dismissed by appeals to accommodation or to any natural limitation of His humanity.

Article XVI.

We affirm that the doctrine of inerrancy has been integral to the Church's faith throughout its history.

We deny that inerrancy is a doctrine invented by scholastic Protestantism, or is a reactionary position postulated in response to negative higher criticism.

Article XVII.

We affirm that the Holy Spirit bears witness to the Scriptures, assuring believers of the truthfulness of God's written Word.

We deny that this witness of the Holy Spirit operates in isolation from or against Scripture.

Article XVIII.

We affirm that the text of Scripture is to be interpreted by grammatico-historical exegesis, taking account of its literary forms and devices, and that Scripture is to interpret Scripture.

We deny the legitimacy of any treatment of the text or quest for sources lying behind it that leads or relativizing, dehistoricizing, or discounting its teaching, or rejecting its claims of authorship.

Article XIX.

We affirm that a confession of the full authority, infallibility and inerrancy of Scripture is vital to a sound understanding of the whole of the Christian faith. We further affirm that such confession should lead to increasing conformity to the image of Christ.

We deny that such confession is necessary for salvation. However, we further deny that inerrancy can be rejected without grave consequences, both to the individual and to the Church.

III. EXPOSITION

Our understanding of the doctrine of inerrancy must be set in the context of the broader teachings of Scripture concerning itself. This exposition gives an account of the outline of doctrine from which our Summary Statement and Articles are drawn.

A. Creation, Revelation and Inspiration

The God, who formed all things by his creative utterances and governs all things by His Word of decree, made mankind in His own image for a life of communion with Himself, on the model of the eternal fellowship of loving communication within the Godhead. As God's image-bearer, man was to hear God's Word addressed to him and to respond in the joy of adoring obedience. Over and above God's self-disclosure in the created order and the sequence of events within it, human beings from Adam on have received verbal messages from Him, either directly, as stated in Scripture, or indirectly in the form of part or all of Scripture itself.

When Adam fell, the Creator did not abandon mankind to final judgement, but promised salvation and began to reveal Himself as Redeemer in a sequence of historical events centering on Abraham's family and culminating in the life, death, resurrection, present heavenly ministry and promised return of Jesus Christ. Within this frame God has from time to time spoken specific words of judgement and mercy, promise and command, to sinful human beings, so drawing them into a covenant relation of mutual commitment between Him and them in which He blesses them with gifts of grace and they bless Him in responsive adoration. Moses, whom God used as mediator to carry his words to His people at the time of the exodus, stands at the head of a long line of prophets in whose mouths and writings God put His words for delivery to Israel. God's purpose in this succession of messages was to maintain His covenant by causing His people to know His name—that is, His nature—and His will both of precept and purpose in the present and for the future. This line of prophetic spokesmen from God came to completion in Jesus Christ, God's incarnate Word, who was Himself a prophet—more that a prophet, but not less—and in the apostles and prophets of the first Christian generation. When God's final and climactic message, His word to the world concerning Jesus Christ, had been spoken and elucidated by those in the apostolic circle, the sequence of revealed messages ceased. Henceforth the Church was to live and know God by what He had already said, and said for all time.

At Sinai God wrote the terms of His covenant on tablets of stone as His enduring witness and for lasting accessibility, and throughout the period of prophetic and apostolic revelation He prompted men to write the messages given to and through them, along with celebratory records of His dealings with His people, plus moral reflections on covenant life and forms of praise and prayer for covenant mercy. The theological reality of inspiration in the producing of Biblical documents corresponds to that of spoken prophecies: Although the human writers' personalities were expressed in what they wrote, the words were divinely constituted. Thus what Scripture says, God says; its authority is His authority, for He is its ultimate Author, having given it through the minds and words of chosen and prepared men who in freedom and faithfulness "spoke from God as they were carried along by the Holy Spirit" (2 Pet. 1:21). Holy Scripture must be acknowledged as the Word of God by virtue of its divine origin.

B. Authority: Christ and the Bible

Jesus Christ, the Son of God who is the Word made flesh, our Prophet, Priest and King, is the ultimate Mediator of God's communication to man, as He is of all God's gifts of grace. The revelation He gave was more than verbal; He revealed the Father by His presence and His deeds as well. Yet His words were crucially important ; for He was God, He spoke from the Father, and His words will judge all men at the last day.

As the prophesied Messiah, Jesus Christ is the central theme of Scripture. The Old Testament looked ahead to Him; the New Testament looks back to His first coming and on to His second. Canonical Scripture is the divinely inspired and there-fore normative witness to Christ. No hermeneutic, therefore, of which the historical Christ is not the focal point is acceptable. Holy Scripture must be treated as what it essentially is—the witness of the Father to the incarnate Son.

It appears that the Old Testament canon had been fixed by the time of Jesus. The New Testament canon is likewise now closed, inasmuch as no new apostolic witness to the historical Christ can now be borne. No new revelation (as distinct from

195

Spirit-given understanding of existing revelation) will be given until Christ comes again. The canon was created in principle by divine inspiration. The Church's part was to discern the canon that God had created, not to devise one of its own.

The word 'canon', signifying a rule of standard, is a pointer to authority, which means the right to rule and control. Authority in Christianity belongs to God in His revelation, which means, on the one hand, Jesus Christ, the living Word, and, on the other hand, Holy Scripture, the written Word. But the authority of Christ and that of Scripture are one. As our Prophet, Christ testified that Scripture cannot be broken. As our Priest and King, He devoted His earthly life to fulfilling the law and the prophets, even dying in obedience to the words of messianic prophecy. Thus as He saw Scripture attesting Him and His authority, so by His own submission to Scripture He attested its authority. As He bowed to His Father's instruction given in His Bible (our Old Testament), so He requires His disciples to do—not, however, in isolation but in conjunction with the apostolic witness to Himself that He undertook to inspire by his gift of the Holy Spirit. So Christians show themselves faithful servants of their Lord by bowing to the divine instruction given in the prophetic and apostolic writings that together make up our Bible.

By authenticating each other's authority, Christ and Scripture coalesce into a single fount of authority. The Biblically-interpreted Christ and the Christ-centered, Christ-proclaiming Bible are from this standpoint one. As from the fact of inspiration we infer that what Scripture says, God says, so from the revealed relation between Jesus Christ and Scripture we may equally declare that what Scripture says, Christ says.

C. Infallibility, Inerrancy, Interpretation

Holy Scripture, as the inspired Word of God witnessing authoritatively to Jesus Christ, may properly be called 'infallible' and 'inerrant'. These negative terms have a special value, for they explicitly safeguard crucial positive truths.

'Infallible' signifies the quality of neither misleading nor being misled and so safeguards in categorical terms the truth that Holy Scripture is a sure, safe and reliable rule and guide in all matters.

Similarly, 'inerrant' signifies the quality of being free from all falsehood or mistake and so safeguards the truth that Holy Scripture is entirely true and trustworthy in all its assertions.

We affirm that canonical Scripture should always be interpreted on the basis that it is infallible and inerrant. However, in determining what the God-taught writer is asserting in each passage, we must pay the most careful attention to its claims and character as a human production. In inspiration, God utilized the culture and conventions of his penman's milieu, a milieu that God controls in His sovereign providence; it is misinterpretation to imagine otherwise.

So history must be treated as history, poetry as poetry, hyperbole and metaphor as hyperbole and metaphor, generalization and approximation as what they are, and so forth. Differences between literary conventions in Bible times and in ours must also be observed: Since, for instance, nonchronological narration and imprecise citation were conventional and acceptable and violated no expectations in those days, we must not regard these things as faults when we find them in Bible writers. When total precision of a particular kind was not expected nor aimed at, it is no error not to have achieved it. Scripture is inerrant, not in the sense of being absolutely precise by modern standards, but in the sense of making good its claims and achieving that measure of focused truth at which its authors aimed.

The truthfulness of Scripture is not negated by the appearance in it of irregularities of grammar or spelling, phenomenal descriptions of nature, reports of false statements (for example, the lies of Satan), or seeming discrepancies between one passage and another. It is not right to set the so-called "phenomena" of Scripture against the teaching of Scripture about itself. Apparent inconsistencies should not be ignored. Solution of them, where this can be convincingly achieved, will encourage our faith, and where for the present no convincing solution is at hand we shall significantly honor God by trusting His assurance that His Word is true, despite these appearances, and by maintaining our confidence that one day they will be seen to have been illusions.

Inasmuch as all Scripture is the product of a single divine mind, interpretation must stay within the bounds of the analogy of Scripture and eschew hypotheses that would correct one Biblical passage by another, whether in the name of progressive revelation or of the imperfect enlightenment of the inspired writer's mind.

Although Holy Scripture is nowhere culture-bound in the sense that its teaching lacks universal validity, it is sometimes culturally conditioned by the customs and conventional views of a particular period, so that the application of its principles today calls for a different sort of action.

D. Skepticism and Criticism

Since the Renaissance, and more particularly since the Enlightenment, world views have been developed that involve skepticism about basic Christian tenets. Such are the agnosticism that denies that God is knowable, the rationalism that denies that He is incomprehensible, the idealism that denies that He is transcendent, and the existentialism that denies rationality in His relationships with us. When these un- and anti-Biblical principles seep into men's theologies at presuppositional level, as today they frequently do, faithful interpretation of Holy Scripture becomes impossible.

E. Transmission and Translation

Since God has nowhere promised an inerrant transmission of Scripture, it is necessary to affirm that only the autographic text of the original documents was inspired and to maintain the need of textual criticism as a means of detecting any slips that may have crept into the text in the course of its transmission. The verdict of this science, however, is that the Hebrew and Greek text appears to be amazingly well preserved, so that we are amply justified in affirming, with the Westminster Confession, a singular providence of God in this matter and in declaring that the authority of Scripture is in no way jeopardized by the fact that the copies we possess are not entirely error-free.

Similarly, no translation is or can be perfect, and all translations are an additional step away from the autograph. Yet the verdict of linguistic science is that English-speaking Christians, at least, are exceedingly well served in these days with a host of excellent translations and have no cause for hesitating to conclude that the true Word of God is within their reach. Indeed, in view of the frequent repetition in Scripture of the main matters with which it deals and also of the Holy Spirit's constant witness to and through the Word, no serious translation of Holy Scripture will so destroy its meaning as to render it unable to make its reader "wise for salvation through faith in Christ Jesus" (2 Tim. 3:15).

F. Inerrancy and Authority

In our affirmation of the authority of Scripture as involving its total truth, we are consciously standing with Christ and His apostles, indeed with the whole Bible and with the main stream of Church history from the first days until very recently. We are concerned at that casual, inadvertent and seemingly thoughtless way in which a belief of such far-reaching importance has been given up by so many in our day.

We are conscious too that great and grave confusion results from ceasing to maintain the total truth of the Bible whose authority one professes to acknowledge. The result of taking this step is that the Bible that God gave loses its authority, and what has authority instead is a Bible reduced in content according to the demands of one's critical reasoning and in principle reducible still further once one has started. This means that at bottom independent reason now has authority, as opposed to Scriptural teaching. If this is not seen and if for the time being basic evangelical doctrines are still held, persons denying the full truth of Scripture may claim an evangelical identity while methodologically they have moved away from the evangelical principle of knowledge to an unstable subjectivism, and will find it hard not to move further.

We affirm that what Scripture says, God says. May He be glorified.

Amen and Amen.

ENDNOTES

Chapter 1: What Does God's Word Mean to Us?

1. "The Chicago Statement on Biblical Inerrancy" finalized at a summit meeting of the International Council on Biblical Inerrancy, held in Chicago, Illinois in October 1978. Chairman was James M. Boice. Council members were: Gleason L. Archer, James M. Boice, Edmund P. Clowney, Norman L. Geisler, John H. Gerstner, Jay H. Grimstead, Harold W. Hoehner, Donald E. Hoke, A. Wetherell Johnson, Kenneth S. Kantzer, James I. Packer, J. Barton Payne, Robert D. Preus, Earl D. Radmacher, Francis A. Schaeffer and R. C. Sproul.

2. Ibid.

3. Ibid.

4. D. Martyn Lloyd-Jones, "The Authority of the Scripture," *Eternity* (April 1957).

5. Ibid.

6. Ibid.

7. Ibid.

8. Billy Graham, "The Authority of the Scriptures," *Decision* (June 1963).

Chapter 2: Who Can Prove God's Word Is True?

1. John F. MacArthur, *Focus on Fact* (Old Tappan, NJ: Fleming H. Revell Company, 1977), chaps. 7,8,9; Henry Morris, *Many Infallible Proofs* (San Diego, CA: Creation-Life Publishers, 1974); Batsell B. Baxter, *I Believe Because* (Grand Rapids, MI: Baker Book House, 1971); Bernard Ramm, *Protestant Christian Evidences* (Chicago: Moody Press, 1953); Harold Lindsell, *God's Incomparable Word* (Wheaton, IL: Victor Books, 1977); James C. Hefley, *Adventures with God . . . Scientists Who Are Christians* (Grand Rapids, MI: Zondervan Publishing House, 1967), p. 72.

2. Paraphrase of Augustine's words in *De Genesi ad Litteram* as quoted in Fritz Ridenour, *Who Says?* (Glendale, CA: Regal Books, 1967), p. 151.

3. W. F. Albright, *Archaeology and the Religion of Israel* (Baltimore, MD: Johns Hopkins Press, 1956).

4. Ridenour, *Who Says?*, pp. 84, 85.
5. Ibid., p. 85.
6. See for example Millar Burrows, *What Mean These Stones?* (American School of Royal Research, 1977); Donald J. Weisman and Edwin Yamauchi, *Archaeology and the Bible; an Introductory Study* (Grand Rapids, MI: Zondervan Publishing House, 1979); Clifford A. Wilson, *Rocks, Relics and Biblical Reliability* (Grand Rapids, MI: Zondervan Publishing House, 1977).
7. Ridenour, *Who Says?*, pp. 78, 79.
8. D. Martyn Lloyd-Jones, "Authority of the Scriptures," *Decision* (June 1963).

Chapter 3: How Did God Inspire His Word?

1. Donald Grey Barnhouse, "When God Breathed," *Eternity* (1961), p. 15.
2. Norman L. Geisler and William E. Nix, *A General Introduction to the Bible* (Chicago: Moody Press, 1968), chaps. 12, 14.
3. J. I. Packer, *God Has Spoken: Revelation and the Bible* (London: Hodden and Stoughton, 1965), p. 81.
4. William Hendriksen, *First and Second Timothy and Titus*, New Testament Commentary Series (Grand Rapids, MI: Baker Book House, 1957), pp. 301, 302.
5. Gordon R. Lewis, "The Human Authorship of Inspired Scripture," *Summit Papers*, International Council on Biblical Inerrancy (1978).
6. For further reading on this subject see: Clark Pinnock, *Biblical Revelation* (Chicago: Moody Press, 1971); Harold Lindsell, *God's Incomparable Word* (Wheaton, IL: Victor Books, 1977); James M. Boice, ed., *The Foundation of Biblical Authority* (Grand Rapids, MI: Zondervan Publishing House, 1978); Thomas A. Thomas, *The Doctrine of the Word of God* (Nutley, NJ: Presbyterian and Reformed Publishing Co., 1972); Benjamin B. Warfield, *The Inspiration and Authority of the Bible* (Nutley, NJ: Presbyterian and Reformed Publishing Co., 1970); Rene Pache, *The Inspiration and Authority of Scripture* (Chicago: Moody Press, 1971); Robert L. Saucy, *The Bible: Breathed from God* (Wheaton, IL: Victor Books, 1978).

Chapter 4: What Did Jesus Think of God's Word?

1. D. Martyn Lloyd-Jones, *Authority* (Downers Grove, IL: Inter-Varsity, 1958), p. 17.

2. Ibid., p. 19.
3. Robert P. Lightner, *The Saviour and the Scriptures* (Nutley, NJ: Presbyterian and Reformed Publishing Co., 1973), p. 83.
4. F. F. Bruce, *The Books and the Parchments* (London: Pickering and Inglis, 1950), p. 164.
5. R. T. France, *Jesus and the Old Testament* (London: Tyndale House Publishers, 1971), p. 27.
6. James I. Packer, *Fundamentalism and the Word of God* (Grand Rapids, MI: Wm. B. Eerdmans Publishing Co., 1958), pp. 54–62.
7. Norman L. Geisler and William E. Nix, *A General Introduction to the Bible* (Chicago: Moody Press, 1968), pp. 59, 60.
8. John M. M'Clintock and James Strong, "Accommodation," *Cyclopaedia of Biblical, Theological-Ecclesiastical Literature* (New York: Arno Press, 1969), vol. l, p. 47.
9. Milton S. Terry, *Biblical Hermeneutics* (Grand Rapids, MI: Zondervan, 1974), p. 166.
10. Geisler and Nix, *General Introduction*, p. 60.
11. Ibid., p. 61.
12. Lightner, *The Saviour and the Scriptures*, p. 47.
13. Packer, *Fundamentalism*, p. 61.
14. For a good discussion of Jesus' promise of divine inspiration to the authors of the New Testament, see Rene Pache, *The Inspiration and Authority of Scripture* (Chicago: Moody Press, 1969), pp. 90–91.

Chapter 5: Can We Add to God's Word?

1. Henry M. Morris, *Many Infallible Proofs* (San Diego, CA: Creation-Life Publishers, 1974), p. 157.
2. Ibid., p. 159.
3. G. Abbot-Smith, *Manual Greek Lexicon of the New Testament* (Edinburgh: T. and T. Clark, 1921), p. 230.
4. Merril C. Tenney, *The New Testament* (Grand Rapids, MI: Wm. B. Eerdmans Publishing Co., 1953), p. 47.
5. B. F. Wescot, *A General Survey of the History of the Canon of the New Testament* (London: Macmillan Publishing Company, Inc., 1875), p. 516.
6. For a full discussion of the development of the Old Testament canon, read Norman L. Geisler and William E. Nix, *From God to Us: How We Got Our Bible* (Chicago: Moody Press, 1974), chap. 7.

7. See Donald Guthrie, "The Canon of Scripture," *The New International Dictionary of the Christian Church* (Grand Rapids, MI: Zondervan Publishing House, 1974), pp. 189–190.
8. For a good discussion of the apocryphal books, see Norman L. Geisler and William E. Nix, *A General Introduction to the Bible* (Chicago: Moody Press, 1976), pp. 162–207.
9. Alma 5:45–46, *The Book of Mormon* (Salt Lake City, UT: The Church of Jesus Christ of Latter-day Saints, 1950), p. 208.
10. *The Christian Science Journal*, vol. 3, no. 7, July, 1975, p. 362.
11. Ibid., p. 361.
12. *The First Church of Christ, Scientist and Miscellany* (Boston, 1941), p. 115.
13. *The Watchtower* (April 15, 1943), p. 127.
14. *Christianity Today*, vol. 21, no. 10 (February 18, 1977), p. 18.

Chapter 6: God's Word: Source of Truth and Freedom

1. See William Hendriksen, *Exposition of the Gospel According to John*, New Testament Commentary (Grand Rapids, MI: Baker Book House, 1953), vol. 2, pp. 50–52.
2. For passages on God as Creator, see Genesis 1:1; Nehemiah 9:6; Job 26:7. For passages on God as Creator of man, see Genesis 1:26–27; Job 12:10. For the eternity of God, see Job 36:26; Psalm 9:7; Ephesians 3:21; 1 Timothy 1:17. For God's faithfulness, see Psalms 100:5; 103:17; 121:3; 1 Corinthians 10:13; 2 Corinthians 1:20; 1 Thessalonians 5:24. For passages on the brevity of life, see 1 Samuel 23; Job 8:9; Psalm 90:9. For everlasting life, see 1 John 2:25; John 5:24; 11:25. For verses on death, see Romans 5:12; 1 Corinthians 15:21–22; Hebrews 9:27.
3. For relationships between men and women and husbands and wives, see the Sermon on the Mount—Matthew 5, 6, 7; 1 Corinthians 7; Ephesians 5:21–33. For relationships between friends and enemies, see Proverbs 17:17; 27:10; 27:17; John 15:13; Matthew 5:43–44.
4. For what the Bible teaches concerning what to eat and drink, see 1 Corinthians 10:31; Romans 14:17–21. For key passages on how to live, see Luke 6:31; Galatians 5:22–26; Romans 12. For verses on how to think, see Philippians 4:6–8; Romans 12:3; Proverbs 12:5.

Chapter 7: God's Word: Guide to His Will

1. Alan Redpath, *Getting to Know the Will of God* (Downers Grove, IL: InterVarsity Press, 1954), p. 12.

2. James C. Dobson, *Dr. James Dobson Talks About God's Will* (Glendale, CA: Regal Books, 1975).
3. Dwight L. Carlson, *Living God's Will* (Old Tappan, NJ: Fleming H. Revell Company, 1976), part 3.
4. Jim Conway, *Mid-Life Crisis* (Elgin, IL: David C. Cook Publishing Company, 1978). Chapters dealing particularly with sexual problems include 10, 11, 15-19.
5. Barbara R. Fried, *The Middle-Age Crisis* (New York: Harper and Row Publishers, Inc., 1967), p. 39.
6. Harold L. Fickett, Jr., is author of several books on Christian living, including: *Keep On Keeping On!* 1 and 2 Thessalonians (Glendale, CA: Regal Books, 1977); *Peter's Principles*, 1 and 2 Peter (Glendale, CA: Regal Books, 1974); *Faith that Works,* James (Glendale, CA: Regal Books, 1972).
7. John F. MacArthur, *Found: God's Will* (Wheaton,lL: Victor Books, 1973).

Chapter 8: God's Word: The Way to Grow

1. William Barclay, *The Letters of James and Peter*, the Daily Study Bible (Edinburgh: The Saint Andrew Press, 1958), pp. 224-226.

Chapter 9: God's Word: The Perfect Pruning Knife

1. Donald Guthrie, *The New Bible Commentary* rev. ed. (Grand Rapids, MI: Wm. B. Eerdmans, © 1970), p. 959.
2. William Barclay, *The Gospel of John, the Daily Study Bible* (Edinburgh: The Saint Andrew Press, 1955), pp. 172-176.
3. Some theologians have misconstrued the analogy of the vine and the branches to conclude that because the vinedresser, the Father, is a detached person who tends the vine, this proves that Christ was not a part of the Godhead. They argue that if Jesus' deity were genuine, the Father would have been represented as something like the roots of the vine. But the point of Jesus' analogy is not to teach anything about His union with the Father. John has already stated quite conclusively that Jesus is God in several other places in his Gospel (see, for example, John 14:1-6). What Jesus is teaching here is the Father's care for the disciples of the Son.
4. For an excellent discussion of things that sometimes pass for fruit, see James E. Rosscup, *Abiding in Christ: Studies in John 15* (Grand Rapids, MI: Zondervan Publishing House, 1973), pp. 70-77.

5. Question 1 of the Westminster Confession: "What is the chief end of man?" The answer: "Man's chief end is to glorify God and enjoy Him forever"—Westminster Assemblies Shorter Catechism.

Chapter 10: God's Word: The Ultimate Weapon

1. For discussion of the Greek words *romphaia* and *machaira*, see W. E. Vine, *Expository Dictionary of New Testament Words* (Old Tappan, NJ: Fleming H. Revell Co., 1940), vol. 4, p. 100.
2. William Barclay, *The Gospel of Matthew*, the Daily Study Bible (Edinburgh: The Saint Andrew Press, 1956). vol. 1, p. 60.
3. A. Naismith, *1200 Notes, Quotes and Anecdotes* (Chicago: Moody Press, 1962), p. 15.

Chapter 11: What Does God's Word Say?

1. Charles R. Pfeiffer and Everett F. Harrison, eds., *The Wycliffe Bible Commentary* (Chicago: Moody Press, 1962), p. 62.
2. For more on a basic Bible reading plan, see Henry H. Halley, *Halley's Bible Handbook*, 24th ed. (Grand Rapids, MI: Zondervan Publishing House, 1965), pp. 805–813.
3. For information on the Navigator's Topical System, see Guidebooks One, Two, and Three. Nav. Press, P.O. Box 20, Colorado Springs, Colorado 80901.

Chapter 12: What Does God's Word Mean (and What Do I Do About It)?

1. For helpful discussion on allegories and other symbolic language in Scriptures, see A. Berkeley Mickelsen and Alvera M. Mickelsen, *Better Bible Study* (Glendale, CA: Regal Books, 1977), chap. 7, "Why Does the Bible Use Figurative Language?" and chap. 12, "What Is an Allegory?"
2. Charles Caldwell Ryrie, *The Ryrie Study Bible*, New Testament (Chicago: Moody Press, 1976).

Made in the USA
Las Vegas, NV
11 June 2021

24537941R00121